eat with your hands
sushi for kids

First published 2013 by
New Holland Publishers Pty Ltd
London • Sydney • Cape Town • Auckland

Garfield House 86–88 Edgware Road London W2 2EA United Kingdom
Wembley Square First Floor Solan Road Gardens Cape Town 8001 South Africa
1/66 Gibbes Street Chatswood NSW 2067 Australia
218 Lake Road Northcote Auckland New Zealand

www.newhollandpublishers.com

A record of this book is held at the British Library and the National Library of Australia

ISBN 9781742572826

Publisher: Fiona Schultz
Designer: Tracy Loughlin
Proofreader: Vicky Fisher
Project editor: Jodi De Vantier
Photographs: Graeme Gillies unless otherwise stated
Cover photos: Keiko Dekura
Production director: Olga Dementiev
Printer: Toppan Leefung Printing Ltd (China)

10 9 8 7 6 5 4 3 2 1

Keep up with New Holland Publishers on Facebook
www.facebook.com/NewHollandPublishers

eat with your hands
sushi for kids

NEW
HOLLAND

Hideo Dekura

Acknowledgements

Having grown up in a family that ran a restaurant, from a very early age I was required to be involved in all sorts of home duties, including many tasks relating to cooking. Meal preparation and cooking became just part of our family's way of life—I was not conscious of having been taught to cook. With eight children in the family, everyone had to contribute.

Looking back over my adult son's life, I now realise that with me as a single parent, he didn't have those same opportunities. With just the two of us, I tended to cook by myself, always in a hurry, more easily in control. It didn't occur to me to take the time to involve him in cooking. I somehow thought that he would automatically do it. Of course, being a chef, I always cooked delicious meals for us, and he enjoys eating, but has never really learned to cook, and I regret not teaching him. I feel we have both lost something by letting that opportunity slip by.

Maybe I see things differently now as I have a wife and a four-year old daughter Yuzuka, who loves food. As a baby, she seemed to use her sense of smell to discover and verify her world. She loves to be around my wife in the kitchen, watching and doing what my wife is doing. Consequently, my wife gives Yuzuka small jobs such as stirring, licking the spatula, cracking eggs, kneading dough, measuring and weighing, filling dumplings etc. Yuzuka's eyes glisten with delight as she confidently says 'I can do it', though her early attempts often resulted in quite a mess. The mess is worth it, when I see how her confidence has grown, and her sense of fulfilment is plainly evident. I always feel nervous and tend to be over-protective while little kids are in the kitchen, but luckily my wife, though always safety conscious, is much more relaxed and easy going. She lets Yuzuka sit on a high stool so she can watch what her mother is doing and they talk to each other about the ingredients, and Yuzuka can smell and touch them. I always love her comments after smelling the food.

There are so many aspects to food, not just how it tastes, but how it smells, looks and feels, where it comes from, and how it gets to the plate before us. Food is something that should not be taken for granted. If we want our family to have a greater appreciation and a depth of understanding of food, taking the time to teach them the basics of cooking is truly worthwhile. In the beginning, it is good to set aside a period of time when you know that you will not be feeling pressured, as your patience may be tested. It will be time well spent. Not only will your children learn some cooking techniques, they will also develop a greater appreciation of food in general, of cultures, life and, most importantly, their parents.

Thanks to all those who have helped me complete this book, especially Jill Elias and Keiko. I am also grateful to Judi Crawford and Atsumi Kondou.

Thanks to Claudios Seafoods, Kikkoman Australia Pty Ltd, Breville, Japan Food Corp. (Aust.) Pty Ltd and Sensory Solutions.

Thanks especially to the children who helped out during the photoshoot: Bella Brown, Ben Glixman, Caitlyn Bressett, Ella Ward, Harry Johansson, Lana Adamian, Lloyd Haslam, Natasha and Jake Morrison, Oliver and Eva Hayes, Yuzuka Dekura.

Contents

For little beginners

Since the birth of my little daughter Yuzuka recently, I have been inspired to write this book. She loves eating, but is not up to cooking just yet. However, she loves to learn new things, and I'm always amazed by her curiosity and her desire to know what is going on around her. Rice is one of her favourite foods, and like most kids, she really enjoys the many varieties of sushi. I can see the day when she will be helping us make sushi and I am looking forward to having her as a little cook in our house. With a little encouragement and supervision any child can be a home cook.

In recent times, sushi has become increasingly popular throughout the Western world, but many people think sushi is only a small roll of rice with a savoury filling wrapped in a thin sheet of nori-seaweed. However, there are many different varieties of sushi, each with a different name, according to their shape, size, ingredients or method of making. They have one thing in common, which is the inclusion of short grain rice flavoured with rice vinegar, sugar and salt.

When the word sushi is prefixed by another word, it is usually pronounced 'zushi', such as 'Nigiri-zushi' (hand-moulded sushi).

Some aspects of making sushi might be difficult for kids, such as cooking the rice, or using a sharp knife to cut ingredients or slice fish, but the actual rolling up can be easily managed, especially with a bit of initial help and guidance from an adult, and some special tips I will include in this book. I would like to enable kids not only to learn how to make sushi in the easiest possible way, but to want to explore the many varieties, enjoy the experience, and maybe learn a little about a different culture.

Introduction

Teaching children is not like teaching adults. Children have less skill and experience, and need to follow clear directions, while still having fun. They need a chance to explore cooking without harming themselves or others. In this book, I give basic rules and guidance, adding comments for parents/ guardians to support their children.

The recipes in this book are intended for children from approximately 8 years, with some basic reading ability.

Children are eager to learn, but they can get overexcited and rush into things, so it is easy for them to make mistakes. They are also striving for independence. In order to give them the space and freedom to learn by themselves in a safe, yet productive way they need to develop skills and knowledge, fostered by adult guidance. At the same time, their challenging nature should be respected, as techniques and outcomes seen by children and adults can be perceived quite differently.

Before starting to cook, I recommend you read the recipe together, assemble the ingredients and equipment, prepare yourselves by washing hands, putting on an apron and create a comfortable, secure atmosphere.

I hope this book can give children many happy sushi-making experiences that may become not only happy memories but also the building blocks for the development of a love of cooking.

I'd like to add some advice especially for parents. Try to create a calm, happy atmosphere in the kitchen. The process of cooking should be as enjoyable as the end result of eating what you have cooked. Don't expect your child to become a Master Chef overnight. Making sushi looks easy, but like all other things, it takes time and practice to develop the techniques.

The ability to cook varies depending on age, experience and the individual, so I have included the symbols below as a general guideline for the level of ability required for each recipe.

Symbols

◎ for beginners, without the use of a knife

◎◎ requires the use of a knife or some supervision

◎◎◎ for advanced level, recipes use a knife and/or heat

Adults—before you start

Cooking sushi can be just as much fun as any other cooking. However, there are some matters to keep in mind regarding safety. This is particularly important for young people who may not be aware of the dangers in the kitchen. Before starting, you should remind children that the kitchen is not a playground and that there are some basic things to remember, especially in relation to sharp and dangerous tools, and heat.

Before starting, you should look objectively at your kitchen so you can pre-empt possible accidents. For example, kitchens are designed for adults, so furniture may need to be re-arranged. A suitable stool or chair may be necessary for your child to be at a comfortable working height. Children need to be taught about the dangers of heat. A sharp knife can usually be seen, but heat isn't usually visible. A stove or pot may be hot long after the heat has been turned off. Hot pots should not be picked up with a tea towel, dish cloth, or any damp/wet cloth. Water coming from the tap may still be very hot if the hot tap was turned on beforehand. In the event that your child suffers a burn, you should know beforehand what steps to take.

Knife safety

Even though many children may have been using a knife for dining purposes before starting this book, the sharpness of the knife should be considered before they use one for cooking purposes. The action can be quite different, involving the use of one hand to hold the food, rather than using a fork. A dining knife is less likely to cause serious harm than a cooking knife, which is usually sharper. The sharpness of various knives can be demonstrated to a child by using each knife to cut through something, such as unpeeled banana, a tomato, etc. Given the opportunity to use a knife with sensible instruction and guidance, children can gradually master the ability to use a knife independently.

Make sure you cover the following points regarding knife safety:

- When using knives or other sharp tools, only use them for the required time and purpose. Otherwise, keep them stored safely. Do not run, point or play with knives. Be particularly careful not to swing a knife behind you.
- Do not place knives on the edge of the bench, with the blade facing upwards or protruding over the edge.
- Do not leave knives in the sink. After using them,

wash each knife individually, and put them in a safe place, out of easy reach of young children.

Children—before you start

Whether making sushi or anything else, working in a kitchen can be dangerous. However, if you learn and follow the rules, you can avoid accidents. If you read the recipes and are careful using the materials and equipment, you will have a great time making sushi.

Make sure you listen to what adults tell you, and if there's anything you don't know or understand, ask an adult, even if you've already been told before.

Planning

- Check ingredients to see if you have everything you need.
- Read the recipe. Ask an adult if there are things you don't understand.
- Have a look around the kitchen with an adult to see what might be dangerous; for example, sharp knives, wet or hot surfaces, slippery floors.
- Clear up the bench top, make a space so you can work comfortably and wipe the surface.
- Always wash your hands with soap before you start cooking.
- Put on an apron, or other suitable clothing before you cook. Be neat; neatness will help to avoid accidents. If you have long hair, tie it back.

While cooking

- Always clean or wash your hands before and after handling food, especially raw meat, poultry or seafood.
- To prevent contamination of food, always clean items that were in contact with raw meat and eggs

immediately after using. Do not leave refrigerated items out on the bench for long periods.

- Do not lick mixing spoons or fingers. Put away ingredients after using them. This helps to keep the working space clear and makes cleaning up at the end easier too.
- If you burn yourself, call for help straight away and put the burnt part in cold water.
- When using a knife or other sharp tools, use them only for the required time and purpose.

Using knives

- Knives are not toys.
- Do not run, point or play with knives. Be particularly careful not to swing a knife behind you.
- Do not place knives on the edge of the bench, with the blade facing upwards or protruding over the edge.
- Do not leave knives in the sink. After using them, wash each knife individually, and put it in a safe place.
- Tell any adults immediately if you: cut yourself, burn yourself, see a fire.

Let's talk about sushi

So, what is sushi? Often, we think of sushi as those little rolls of rice wrapped in a piece of dark-greenish, paper-like seaweed, with some tasty fillings such as fish, chicken or vegetables. Sometimes we have seen rice on the outside of those rolls too. And maybe you have even seen different size rolls—big ones and small. If you have been lucky, you may have had sushi from a large sushi platter including decorated sushi, or even pink rice. Maybe you've seen lots of sushi travel past you on a sushi train and it's been hard to choose what to eat—they look so yummy you want to have them all!

The term 'sushi' covers many different kinds of rice and vinegar food, of all shapes and sizes. Some are wrapped in different ingredients, some are not wrapped at all. Each style of sushi has its own Japanese name and these names describe the sushi by its size, shape and ingredients. A word you may have heard is 'zushi'. This is exactly the same as 'sushi' but when 'sushi' is used in a compound (joined) word, it is always pronounced 'zushi'. An example of this is 'chirashi-zushi', which you will learn how to make later. One type of sushi has even managed to get an American name. Can you guess what it is? Of course, it's the California roll. The more often you see and say the Japanese names, the more likely you are to remember them. You don't have to remember the names as long as you know what's in them. Sometimes they are strange to pronounce, as all the vowels are sounded separately, and often don't sound the way English vowels sound.

Here is a description of the main types of sushi, which you will better understand when you start to

make sushi yourself. They are all made with rice that is flavoured with vinegar and usually a little sugar and salt. Traditionally, a small amount of wasabi paste was included in the rolls, but these days, in Western countries, wasabi is often served as an optional extra to be mixed in with some soy sauce as an accompaniment. Some sushi are made to size, others are made larger, usually because of the size of the nori sheets, then cut to size later.

Nori-maki or maki-zushi

Rice rolled in a sheet of dried seaweed, with a filling of various vegetables, egg, seafood or chicken. 'Nori' is the name of the dried seaweed sheet and 'maki' means 'roll'. Nori-maki have different names according to the fillings and their size and shape: *hoso-maki* are thin, *chu-maki* are medium-sized and *futo-maki* are thick rolls.

Uramaki

Also called California roll or inside-out roll, as it has a layer of rice on the outside. It always has avocado in the filling, which was not common in Japan years ago.

Tazuna-zushi (rope/rainbow sushi)

Sushi rice rolled with portions of various ingredients, such as smoked salmon, salad leaves or omelette and placed at an angle so that when it is rolled it looks like a rope.

Nigiri-zushi

A moulded pad of rice topped with seafood. 'Nigiri' means 'pressed in the hand', which is how the sushi

is formed. There are different names depending on the type of seafood used. This sushi is not wrapped in nori (see photo top left).

Gunkan, Battleship sushi

Gunkan is a variation of nigiri-zushi. It is an oval-shaped ball of sushi rice wrapped with nori, with some tasty topping, in a shape that more or less resembles a battleship.

Temari-zushi (ball sushi)

Temari is a traditional Japanese decorative ball, a bit smaller than a golf ball. As sushi, temari-zushi are round balls of rice with a decorative topping.

Inari-zushi

A pocket of deep-fried tofu skin called abura-age, stuffed with rice. Inari is the name of the Fox God (known as *Kitsune*) of rice, agriculture and fertility. It is believed that the Fox God likes to eat abura-age, which is the colour of fox's fur.

Chirashi-zushi (scattered sushi)

Chirashi-zushi is a great one-dish sushi meal that is easy to prepare at home. Chirashi means 'scattered', and this is what you do: fill a bowl with sushi rice and then scatter the ingredients such as prawns, chopped omelette, tuna, white fish, shiitake mushrooms, sesame seeds decoratively over the rice. Or the ingredients can be mixed with the sushi rice. It is served at room temperature.

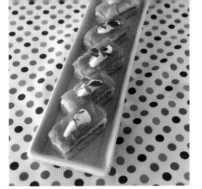

Oshi-zushi (pressed sushi)

Sushi rice pressed into a box mould with other ingredients as a topping or filling. The mould is removed and the rice form cut into bite-sized pieces. There may be pastry cutters in your kitchen, which can be used as a mould. Sometimes the moulded form is wrapped with persimmon or bamboo leaves.

Fukusa-zushi

'Fukusa' is a cloth for wrapping. As sushi, a thin egg crêpe is wrapped around rice and tied up with a string made of vegetable, such as kampyo (dried gourd strip), chives or scallions (spring onions).

Saiku-zushi and matsuri-zushi
(decorative sushi)

This type of sushi is a decorative sushi for special events and festivals. The top of nigiri-zushi or maki-zushi are decorated with a variety of colourful and artistic motifs such as flowers or animals, using the usual sushi toppings in unusual ways.

Temaki-zushi
(hand-wrapped sushi)

Do-it-yourself hand-wrapped cones of nori filled with sushi rice and a variety of ingredients. You can also use other wrap ingredients such as omelettes or rice paper. They make excellent party food. Simply prepare the rice and fillings ahead of time and lay them out attractively in separate bowls or one large platter on the table. Give your guests guidance on how to make the rolls and let them make their own.

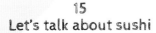
Let's talk about sushi

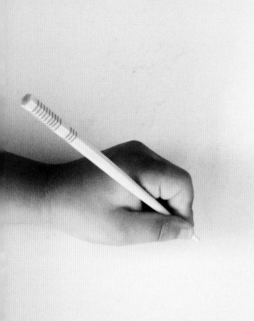

Equipment and Tools

Here is a list of the equipment traditionally used when preparing sushi. You may never have seen some of it before, so I have included alternatives you may have in your own kitchen.

Hangiri (rice-cooling tub)

This is a wide, flat-based wooden tub with low sides, generally made of cypress. It is designed specifically for cooling sushi rice to give the rice the ideal texture and gloss required for Japanese sushi. If you are using a hangiri, wash it well after use, dry it carefully, then wrap it in a cloth and store it face down in a cool, dry place. For a substitute, you may use a wide, wooden bowl.

1
2

Hashi (chopsticks)

There are varieties of hashi, depending on usage, such as waribashi (disposable half-split chopsticks) and sai-bashi (long cooking chopsticks) (hashi is pronounced 'bashi' when used in compound words).

At home in Japan, usually each family member has their own pair of chopsticks, which may have attractive colours and designs.

Traditional Japanese chopsticks have thin pointed ends and come in a range of sizes and shapes, with very small ones for children and long ones for larger men, plus extra long ones for cooking. The ideal chopstick measurement is said to be one and a half times the length from the tip of the thumb to the tip of the index finger when the hand is opened to a right angle (90 degrees) .

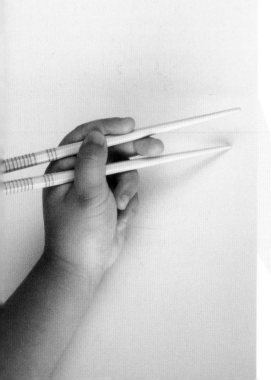

How to hold chopsticks

- Hold a chopstick as if holding a pen (see photo 1, opposite).
- Insert another chopstick between the index finger and middle finger from the base of thumb.
- Line up the points. Grip the lower chopstick firmly at the base of thumb, supported by the first knuckle joint of the ring finger (see photo 2, opposite).
- Move the upper chopstick using thumb and index finger. Try to move only the upper chopstick, not the lower one. Try to touch the point of the upper chopstick to that of the lower one.

At the table

Chopsticks should always be set to point to the left at the table. For formal dining, there is a chopstick rest underneath them. Some people make a chopstick rest out of the paper case when using disposable chopsticks.

Hōcho (knife)

Unlike Western knives, which have a double blade, Japanese knives have a cutting blade on one side only, and a wooden handle. The cutting blade is usually on the right side for right-hand users, but left-hand blades can be ordered.

Traditional Japanese knives need extra care to prevent them from rusting. Nowadays, the most commonly used ones are made from stainless steel, which does not rust.

In this book, only basic slicing skills are needed so a kitchen knife will be suitable, as long as it is sharp.

Choosing a knife

Knives are available for children, but should be used under adult supervision. Make sure you and an adult have read all of the safety rules to do with knives before you start making sushi.

The ideal length of blade for children is about two times longer than a child's clenched fist. Here are some recommended knife sizes for kids (using a petite, vegetable knife or cook's knife):

- 4½in (11.5cm) blade size for 7-year-olds
- 5in (13cm) blade for 7–15-year-olds
- 6⅓in (16cm) blade for 15-year-olds and older

Makisu or maki-sudare (sushi mat)

Makisu is a small mat made of narrow strips of bamboo and it is vital for rolling sushi. Several sizes of makisu are available—some that are wider than a whole nori sheet to much smaller ones. The regular size is about 9½ x 8⅓in (24 x 21cm). For small kids, 5 x 7in (13 x 18cm) size (for temaki-zushi) is available. After using the mat, scrape off any rice with a brush or sponge and dry well. As a substitute, you could use a silicon mat, which is commonly used for dough-making.

Manaita (chopping board)

Use a chopping board that is wide enough to cut on and not too small. When using a chopping board, place a damp cloth or stopper sheet underneath, to keep it steady. After you've finished chopping, wash the board well and stand to dry properly.

Rice cooker

You can cook rice in a pot, but using a rice cooker makes it easier to cook rice without any problems or fuss. However, read the booklet before using and always wipe the bowl with a dry cloth when placing the bowl in the rice cooker. I prefer using a rice cooker, which seals tightly when closed.

Shamoji (spoon)

Shamoji is a spoon to fold or scoop rice. It is made from wood (mostly bamboo) or plastic. Before using it, dampen it in water to prevent rice from sticking all over it. For a substitute, you may use a wooden spatula or a flat spoon.

Tamagoyaki-ki (Japanese omelette pan)

A Japanese omelette pan is not round, but rectangular-shaped and about 1in (3cm) deep.

Tweezers

Tweezers are used for removing fish bones. Japanese tweezers have wide, flat tips designed to efficiently remove fish bones but you can ask your fishmonger or an adult to remove the bones before you start.

Vegetable peeler

The Japanese peeler is similar to a potato peeler, but the blade is set at a right angle to the handle, which makes it easy to slice vegetables in thin, long strips. These strips are used for making wrapper-type sushi.

Other utensils

- Cooking scissors: used for cutting nori, trimming leaves, etc.
- Scales and measuring cups and spoons
- Bowls
- Saucepans
- Slicer: to use for slicing vegetables
- Spatula: instead of shamoji (a rice spoon) a spatula is used for folding rice or mixing sushi rice
- Strainer: to strain rice, etc.
- Vegetable or cookie cutter: to cut vegetables, etc.
- Moulds: to prepare moulded sushi with other ingredients. Also small cake tins could be used as moulds.
- Uchiwa (hand fan): These plastic fans are used to cool down rice when preparing sushi rice.
- Deep-fryer: Get an adult to help you when you need to deep-fry tempura or crumbed chicken or potatoes.

Essential Ingredients for Sushi

Kome (rice)

Rice (flavoured with a little rice vinegar, sugar and salt) is the basic ingredient for sushi. There are many different varieties of rice. They all look slightly different when they are raw but, most importantly, when they are cooked they have different flavours and other characteristics too. For sushi, the best type is medium or short-grain Japonica rice. It has a good flavour, and it is more glutinous than other types, which means that when it's cooked, it will retain more moisture and be a bit more sticky, so that it clumps together lightly. This is what we want when we make sushi, so that the sushi doesn't fall to pieces when we are eating it. Once you have learned how to make sushi with short-grained rice, you may like to experiment with other varieties such as wild rice, black or brown rice (genmai). I have included some recipes to inspire you.

In Japan, people can be very particular about the brand of rice they buy for sushi, but in any country there are always good brands, whether they are imported from Japan or locally grown. Rice should be stored in an airtight container in a dry, cool, dark place. Brown rice will not last as long as white rice because it has a higher oil content.

Remember, when rice is cooked it expands about two and a half times its original volume, so you always end up with more than you started with.

Su (vinegar)

When making sushi it is important to add a small amount of vinegar to the cooked rice while it is still hot. There is a special type of vinegar, which is rice vinegar. There is also pre-made sushi vinegar/seasoning called *awase-zu* (pronounced: ah-wah-se-zoo). It is slightly sweeter than regular rice vinegar. It is mostly sold as a liquid, but is also available in powder form.

Cooked Rice

Ingredients
2 cups short-grain rice
water

Utensils
rice cooker (highly recommended), rice measuring cup (the measuring cup with the rice cooker is usually smaller than 9fl oz (250ml)), strainer, bowl (a little bigger than strainer), dry towel

◎ Method using a rice cooker
When using a rice cooker, use the measuring cup provided. Rice should be rinsed well before cooking.

1. Place a strainer over a bowl just a little bigger than the strainer.
2. Add rice.
3. Add water until it just covers the rice.
4. Hold the strainer with one hand and briskly stir the rice for 10–15 seconds with the other hand.
5. Lift strainer, drain off and discard the milky water.
6. Repeat this twice, stirring for about 15 seconds

after adding the water to remove excess starch.

7. After draining (for the third time), add more water to cover the rice and allow it to soak for 30 minutes.

8. Drain rice well and transfer rice to the rice cooker.

9. Add the recommended amount of water to the rice cooker pan.

10. Wipe the bottom of the pot with a dry towel and set it in the rice cooker. Close lid, turn on and allow to cook.

11. When the rice cooker has turned off, leave for 10 minutes to steam.

12. The hot rice is now ready for the next stage of mixing.

◎◎ Method with Saucepan

Use a stainless steel or non-stick saucepan that has a close-fitting lid.

Ingredients
2 cups short-grain rice
2 cups water

1. Rinse rice 3 times as mentioned in the rice cooker method.

2. Soak the rice in water for 30 minutes.

3. Drain rice and transfer to a saucepan.

4. Add 2 cups cold water.

5. Bring water to the boil over high heat, then put on the lid and turn heat to the lowest setting. Cook for 12 minutes, turn off heat and allow to steam for a further 10 minutes with the lid on. Carefully remove the lid after 10 minutes.

The hot rice is now ready for the next stage of mixing.

◎ Brown Rice

Ingredients
3 cups brown rice
3½ cups water

Utensils
rice cooker (highly recommended), rice measuring cup, strainer, bowl

Basically you do not need to rinse brown rice as much as short grain rice before cooking. However, you need to check that it does not contain small foreign substances such as pebbles or twigs.

1. Place a strainer over a bowl just a little bigger than the strainer.

2. Add rice.

3. Using a cup, add water until it just covers the rice

4. Hold the strainer with one hand and briskly stir the rice for 10-15 seconds with the other hand.

5. Lift strainer, drain off and discard the murky water.

6. After draining, add more water to cover the rice and allow it to soak for at least 1 hour or overnight.

7. Drain rice well and transfer rice to the rice cooker.

8. Add 2½ cups water to the rice cooker pan.

9. Wipe the bottom of the pan with a dry towel and set it in the rice cooker.

Essential ingredients

10. Close lid, turn on and allow to cook.
11. When the rice cooker has turned off, leave for 20 minutes to steam.
12. The hot rice is now ready for the next stage of mixing.
13. When cooking brown rice in a saucepan, you need to cook it for about 40 minutes over low heat without scorching.

Coloured Rice

Ingredients
3 cups short-grain rice
1–2 tablespoons wild rice

Cook coloured rice using the same method as Cooked Rice.

 Sushi Rice

Ingredients
2½fl oz (70ml) rice vinegar
1¾oz (50g) superfine (caster) sugar
a small pinch of salt
3 cups hot cooked short-grain rice (see recipe for Cooked Rice)

NOTE: Pre-made sushi vinegar (*awase-zu*) is also available, either liquid or powder.

Utensils
measuring cup, rice paddle, dry towel or mitten, hangiri (as a substitute for hangiri, a wooden salad bowl is ideal), hand fan, rice paddle or a wooden spatula, muslin cloth or kitchen towel

1. To make sushi vinaigrette, mix rice vinegar, sugar and salt in a cup or bowl, until sugar has dissolved (see photo 1).
2. Moisten the wooden bowl with a damp towel.
3. Using a damp rice paddle, transfer the hot cooked rice into the bowl.
4. Spread rice evenly in the bowl.
5. Gradually pour sushi vinaigrette over the rice (see photo 2).
6. Mix the rice evenly around the bowl with a slicing action (see photo 3).
7. While mixing, cool the rice with a hand fan so that the rice absorbs the vinegar mixture and becomes glossy (see photo 4).
8. Cover with a muslin cloth and let it cool down until slightly warm.

Tip
The rice pot will still be hot when you transfer the rice to the wooden bowl; you may have to ask an adult to help. If you do it by yourself, make sure you use a dry towel or mitten to grip the pan firmly as you spoon the rice into the bowl.

Essential ingredients

◎ Pink Sushi Rice Mixture

Makes about 3 tablespoons of pink rice mixture

Ingredients
2oz (60g) red beetroot
2½fl oz (70ml) rice vinegar
2¼oz (70g) superfine (caster) sugar
a pinch of salt

Utensils
cheese grater with a tray, bowls, strainer
1. Rinse raw beetroot and grate using a cheese grater into a bowl (see photo 1).
2. Add vinegar, sugar and salt and mix well (see photo 2).
3. Strain into another bowl (see photo 3).

Tip
Add this mixture to the warm rice and mix in the same way to make pink sushi rice. You can also freeze any leftover liquid in cubes if you do not use it all.

You can make beetroot jam (see recipe) with the beetroot pulp and use the jam as sushi decoration, sauce or topping.

◎ Pink Sushi Rice

makes 2 cups cooked pink sushi rice

Ingredients
17½oz (500g) cooked sushi rice (see recipe)
1¾–2¼oz (50–70g) pink sushi rice mixture (see recipe)

Utensils
bowl, rice paddle

1. Place sushi rice in a bowl and drizzle pink sushi rice mixture over the rice (see photo 4).
2. Mix everything together with a moist rice paddle, until the rice is evenly coloured (see photo 5 and 6).

◎◎◎ Beetroot Jam

1 teaspoon mirin
2 tablespoons water
¼ cup superfine (caster) sugar
2oz (60g) beetroot pulp (leftover from Pink Sushi Rice Mixture recipe)

Utensils
saucepan, wooden spoon

The leftover beetroot pulp after it has been strained can be used as topping on sushi as a decoration and also taste enhancer. Mirin is only used for cooking but it does contain alcohol.

1. You will need an adult to help you with this step. Place the beetroot in a saucepan and over moderate heat boil down for about 5 minutes or until it becomes thick like jam, stirring constantly at the same time with a wooden spoon (see photo 7 and 8).
2. Cool it down to room temperature and use for toppings (see photo 9).
3. It will keep for one week in the refrigerator.

1

2

3

4

5

6

7

8

9

Japanese Groceries

Abura-age (thinly sliced, deep-fried tōfu)

Abura-age is thin, slightly sweet, flavoured sheets of deep-fried tofu, which are made into little pouches. These pouches are filled with sushi rice to make inari-zushi. They are usually bought already flavoured from the freezer section in Japanese grocery shops, but if you buy them unflavoured you can prepare them yourself. You can also cut them into strips and add them to miso soup.

Aonori (green nori powder)

This coarsely ground nori can be used to sprinkle onto inside-outside sushi rolls and is also used as a coating for tempura.

Cha or o-cha (tea)

See Drinks in Let's Make Sushi section.

Dashi (Japanese stock)

Instead of chicken or beef stock, the Japanese use dashi, their own version of stock. There is a recipe for stock in the Soups part of Let's Make Sushi section. It is also available in powdered form from Asian grocers and some supermarkets.

Denbu (lightly minced fish)

A pink mixture made from white fish with natural colouring, used in chirashi-zushi or as a decoration for sushi rolls or nigiri. It is sometimes called sakura-denbu (cherry denbu) and is sold in small packs.

Furikake (sprinkle-seasoning)

Furikake is a dried condiment that is sprinkled over dishes, especially plain cooked rice. It typically consists of a mixture of some of the following: sesame seeds, ground fish, shredded nori, egg, katsuo-bushi or vegetables. Yukari is a type of furikake made from seasoned dried red shiso. Furikake is used as a decoration for sushi, especially inside-out rolls.

Gari (pickled ginger)

Gari are ginger slices that have been pickled in salt and sweet vinegar. They are a delicate pink colour and are available in bottles or vacuum-packs. Small amounts of gari are eaten between bites of sushi to freshen your mouth, as it is quite tangy.

Sometimes you see bright-red, vinegared ginger, but this is not called gari, it is called beni-shoga. It is not used with sushi, but sometimes with chirashi-zushi (scattered sushi).

◎◎◎ Gari (Pickled Ginger)

makes 7oz (200g)

Ingredients
3½fl oz (100ml) rice vinegar
1½oz (40g) superfine (caster) sugar (if you like

sweeter gari, add extra sugar)
a pinch of salt
7oz (200g) fresh, young ginger (young ginger is a
slightly pinkish, creamy colour and only available
in season from early summer)

Utensils
saucepan, wooden spoon, peeler or slicer (or knife), a container with a lid

1. Combine vinegar, sugar and salt in a pan and stir it over a low heat until sugar is dissolved.
2. Allow to cool down.
3. Using a vegetable peeler or slicer, peel the skin from the ginger and then slice the ginger into paper-thin slices.
4. Soak in cold water for 15 minutes.
5. Rinse and drain well.
6. To reduce bitterness, pour boiling water over ginger, then drain the ginger and squeeze.
7. Pickle in the sweet vinegar mixture overnight in the refrigerator. Transfer the ginger slices to a container with an airtight lid.

Ginger Rose as Garnish
1. Lay 5–6 pieces of gari across a clean chopping board, each one slightly overlapping the piece next to it.
2. Pick up the edge nearest you and roll to the other end.
3. Stand the roll on its end and slightly open the top out so it resembles a rose. Serve as a garnish.

Goma (sesame seeds)
Black and cream/white sesame seeds are commonly found. You can buy them roasted or ask an adult to help you toast them yourself in a dry frying pan over medium heat. Move them around in the pan with a wooden spoon so that they turn golden brown and do not burn. Roasted sesame has a stronger aroma and a darker colour. For sushi, sesame seeds are often used as a final decoration for coating or topping.

Kamaboko (fish cakes)
These Japanese-style fish cakes are available frozen. There are various forms, some of them dyed pink. Kamaboko can be used in chirashi-zushi.

Kampyō (dried gourd shavings)
A gourd is a plant related to cucumbers and marrows. Sliced and dried gourd is used in the form of ribbon-like strips. Before being used in sushi, kampyō is tenderised and seasoned. You can buy it already cooked, but the dried variety is more common in Asian grocery shops.

◎◎◎ Kampyō Preparation for Sushi

Ingredients
2/3oz (20g) dried kampyō
1 cup dashi stock
2 tablespoons superfine (caster) sugar
1½ tablespoons soy sauce

Utensils

bowl, saucepan, strainer, wooden spoon

1. Put some water and a pinch of salt in a bowl and rub the kampyō in the bowl with your hands until it softens.
2. Rinse under running water.
3. Put water in a pan and bring it to the boil. Add kampyō and cook for 10 minutes.
4. Drain and transfer into a bowl of cold water and drain again.
5. Put dashi and sugar in a pan and bring it to the boil.
6. Add kampyō to the dashi and cook over low heat for 5 minutes.
7. Add soy sauce and simmer for about 3 minutes.
8. Cool it down to room temperature.

Kani-kama

An artificial crab-meat stick made of fish paste and other ingredients. It is used as a filling for nori rolls.

Katsuo-bushi (bonito flakes)

Katsuo-bushi is used to make stock for miso soup. It is also used in the preparation of some sushi ingredients such as abura-age for inari-zushi. It is also used as a topping for salads. It is sold in a packet (see Miso Soup recipe).

Mirin (cooking rice wine)

Mirin is a type of sweet sake used in cooking to enrich the flavour of a dish or to glaze the surface of the food when you are grilling. It does contain alcohol but this will cook out when heated.

Miso (fermented soybean paste)

Miso is a tasty ingredient made from fermented soybeans, malt and salt. There are several varieties of miso, which may be distinguished by colour, ingredients and method or area of production. It is used as a basic ingredient in soups, for flavouring in stews and sauces.

Nori (sheets of seaweed)

Used for making sushi rolls. The sheets measure about 7½ x 7¾in (19 x 20cm) and are sold in a packet. Once the wrapping has been opened, use the nori as soon as possible or keep in a closed plastic bag in the fridge. Make sure you buy pre-roasted nori, known as yaki-nori, not the raw type. Nori are smooth on one side, rough on the other. The smooth side goes on the outside of the roll. Nori sheets have a slight linear pattern. This should be aligned with the stitching on the bamboo mat when using the whole nori sheet to make large rolls.

Panko

Panko is a variety of Japanese bread crumbs. It is crispier than Western bread crumbs and is often used on fish or seafood.

Shiitake (shiitake mushrooms)

Fresh or dried shiitake mushrooms are available. Dried shiitake are mainly used to make stock. For sushi, sliced shiitake cooked with soy sauce and sugar are used for rolls or chirashi-zushi.

Shōyu (soy sauce)

Shōyu is the most common accompaniment with sushi. It is a fermented sauce made from soy beans, wheat, salt and water. It can be used as a versatile seasoning, in cooking or as a base for soup. There are various types of soy sauce, depending on ingredients and character. For sushi, choose naturally brewed, not chemically made soy sauce, such as Kikkoman brand soy sauce. Organic soy sauce, low/less-salt soy sauce, tamari soy sauce or gluten-free soy sauce is also suitable.

Takuwan (pickled daikon)

Pickled white radish, also known as daikon, is called *takuwan*. There are several varieties and colours of *takuwan*, but the most common one used for sushi rolls is yellow *takuwan*. It is sold whole or halved in a packet.

Tobiko (flying fish roe)

See Fish section.

Tofu (soybean curd)

A white curd of custard-like texture made from soy beans, which can be added to miso soup. For soup, use the Japanese 'silken' variety. Tofu must be kept in the refrigerator, in water deep enough to cover it. Once opened, change the water at least twice a day. Stored this way, tofu will last a couple of days, but it is best used straight after opening.

Umeboshi (pickled dried ume-plums)

The Japanese plums, *ume-boshi*, can be large or small, hard or soft. After being dried, they are usually pickled with salt and coloured red by being preserved with red shiso leaves. They are sold in a packet, either with pits or pitted, or even as a paste in a tube or bottle.

The large ones can be used for sushi rolls when the seed is removed. The taste may be very salty and tangy, though less salty, somewhat sweeter ones are also now available. They are good when combined with other ingredients and are used in dressings and sauces as well.

Wakame (wakame-seaweed)

Wakame is a type of seaweed available in dried form and often used in miso soup. Dried wakame must be soaked before using.

Wasabi (Japanese green horseradish)

A native Japanese plant that is found growing near clear spring water. Fresh wasabi has a lovely texture, distinctive pungent tang and aroma. However, fresh wasabi is expensive and largely unavailable outside Japan, so powdered wasabi, which is mixed with a small amount of tepid water to make a paste, is more common. In Japan, a small amount of wasabi is usually included in the sushi, but for kids, wasabi is too spicy and hot to use in sushi. When it is served separately, it can be mixed with a little soy sauce.

Other ingredients

Other than Japanese groceries, you can use these general ingredients for sushi: ham, cheese, chicken, smoked salmon, eggs, mayonnaise—try whatever you like!

Vegetables and Herbs

Fresh vegetables are great fillings for sushi and for making decorations when you serve the sushi. Vegetables are eaten raw or blanched, or sometimes cooked with extra flavouring, such as soy sauce. Try some of these vegetables in your sushi:

- asparagus spears
- avocado
- bell peppers (capsicums)
- carrots
- corn
- cucumber (Lebanese cucumber is suitable)
- English spinach, fresh or blanched
- green beans/French beans
- green salad leaves
- lettuce
- lotus root (renkon), cooked
- mizuna leaves
- okra
- red radish
- scallions (spring onions)
- snow peas and snow pea sprouts
- tomato
- watercress
- white daikon (white radish)

Herbs

Shiso (Japanese basil)

Shiso is a Japanese summer herb with a pleasant aroma. It is used raw, not only sliced finely with food, but also decoratively as a whole leaf. There are two types, the green and the red, but the green shiso is most commonly used. Dried shiso is called yukari and is available as a sushi sprinkle topping.

Sometimes we can find shiso plants sold at nursery shops. You can grow it easily at home in your garden or in planters. You can buy shiso from Japanese groceries during summer.

You can also use these non-Japanese herbs in sushi:
- cilantro (coriander)
- mint

Fish and Seafood

Filleting a whole fish is not easy for children, or even for adults. You may be able to purchase a packet of salmon, king-fish or tuna block that is of sashimi quality (that is raw fish), pre-cut for sushi, which is very convenient. These fish are suitable for sushi:

Buri (king fish)

This is a long, slender fish covered with tiny round scales. The back is dark green and the belly part is silvery white. In the centre there is a yellow line, which runs the length of the body. They come as big as 33lb (15kg), but you can buy sashimi-quality filleted kingfish.

Maguro (tuna)

Tuna is one of the most popular fish for sushi because of its rich red colour and full-bodied flavour. Purchase only a block the size you need, and check that the flesh is firm.

Salmon

The orange colour of salmon is very attractive on a plate. If salmon is unavailable, substitute ocean trout. Smoked salmon is handy too for using in sushi-rolls or chirashi-zushi (scattered sushi). Salmon caviar is expensive but small amounts can be used as a garnish for nigiri-zushi (hand-moulded sushi), chirashi-zushi (scattered sushi) or gunkan (battleship sushi).

Unagi (eel)

Filleting eel is quite difficult even for adults so it is better to purchase flavoured grilled eel in an airtight plastic pack from the freezer section of Japanese grocery shops. When using, follow the directions on the packet.

Eel is used for nigiri-zushi, chirashi-zushi and nori-rolls.

Other seafood

Caviar (salmon roe)

Used for decoration or gunkan (battleship sushi).

Ebi (jumbo shrimp/king prawns)

This is one of the most popular seafoods for sushi.

Ika (squid)

If using raw squid, they should be sashimi quality. Ika is often used for nigiri-zushi.

Tobiko (flying fish roe)

Tobiko is used for decoration, especially for inside-out rolls. Orange-coloured tobiko is common, but green and golden ones are also available.

Other products

Canned tuna, canned salmon, canned crabmeat, crabmeat stick.

Fish and seafood

Slicing Fish Fillets

To slice fish for sushi topping, it is best to start with a rectangular block of fish about the width of your hand, measuring about 2¼in (6cm) across and 1½in (4cm) high. Of course, the block you have purchased will not be cut to these measurements, so it will need to be cut. A large fish, such as tuna, may be easy to cut. With other fish, such as salmon, try to cut the fish into a block, although the ends and sides may not be very even. With salmon or white fish, you can often cut following the existing angle of the fillet.

First slice off a triangular piece to make an angled edge to work with (any scraps can be used in rolled sushi).

With your knife on a slant to match the angle of the working edge of the block, cut slices about ⅛in (3-4mm) thick. The last piece of the block will also be triangular.

The method is also used with smaller filleted fish, adjusting the knife angle to suit the fillet. With fish such as tuna the resulting slices will be uniform and rectangular. With smaller fillets, you may have triangular edges or thinner slices. Sometimes you may need to use more than one slice for a piece of nigiri-zushi.

Preparing Jumbo Shrimp (King Prawns) for Sushi Toppings

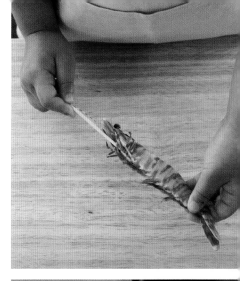

Ingredients

6 jumbo shrimp (king prawns)
pinch of salt
½ cup rice vinegar
¼ cup water
1 tablespoon superfine (caster) sugar

Utensils

bamboo skewers, saucepan, chopping board, small knife, tray or bowl

1. In salt water (about 36fl oz/1 litre and a pinch of salt), rinse raw seafood and wipe with kitchen paper.
2. To keep the shrimp from curling during parboiling, pierce with skewers along the belly side from head to tail (see photo 1).
3. Bring some water to boil in a saucepan and add a pinch of salt. Simmer prawns for 3 minutes over moderate heat, then plunge into a bowl of cold water. Remove skewers. Remove shells from prawns, but leave tails intact. Devein (remove the vein running along the back) using a small knife (see photo 2).
4. Place shrimp on a chopping board and, with a small knife, make a slit on the belly side to open up like a butterfly then gently flatten out.
5. Combine vinegar, water and sugar in a tray or bowl and place prawns in this mixture until ready to use (see photo 3).

These can be used in recipes for:
Shrimp (Prawn) Tempura (see recipe)
Shrimp (Prawn) in Breadcrumbs (see recipe)

Basic Techniques

Garnishes and Decorations

Shredded nori: Used for topping such as chirashi-zushi (scattered sushi). Fold up a sheet of nori and cut it into long thin slices.

Plastic fish soy bottles: For picnics or in a lunch box, these disposable small bottles are useful. You can purchase them from Japanese grocery shops. You can keep the bottles when you purchase takeaway sushi as they can be easily refilled. Firstly, put some soy sauce into a small bowl. Insert the top opening part of the bottle into the soy sauce, squeeze out the air, and release your finger pressure to suck up the fluid.

Egg mimosa: It is used for decoration on sushi or flower-shaped carved vegetables.

Egg mimosa
Makes 1 tablespoon egg mimosa

Ingredients
1 egg

Utensils
saucepan, bowl, strainer, spoon

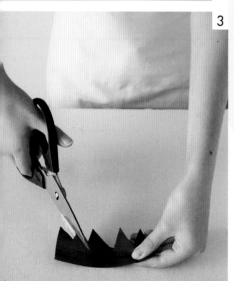

1. Place an egg gently in a saucepan of water.
2. Bring it to the boil and cook until hard-boiled, about 15 minutes.
3. Allow egg to cool. Remove shell and egg white and take out egg yolk. Place the yolk into a fine strainer and, using a spoon, sieve the yolk through the strainer into a small container (see photo 1 and 2).

Green leaves, such as camellia leaf, bamboo, haran:
Camellia leaf, bamboo leaves are used only for garnishing sushi, either to make the dish look pretty or to give the dish some colour when you serve it. Adults can cut these with a knife. Otherwise, use cooking scissors to cut out shapes (see photo 3).

Flower-shaped vegetables: Use a vegetable or cookie cutter, to cut sliced vegetables into various shapes. Some vegetables are very hard to cut, but if you use a towel to cover the cutter it makes it easier.

Radishes and Cucumbers: Vegetables such as radishes, carrots and cucumber can be decoratively carved for use as garnishes. When deciding which garnish is best suited for your sushi, consider the colours of other ingredients. Flowers, leaves and other designs drawn from nature are traditionally used. Remember that these carved vegetables should not be the main element on the plate.

Red Radish Flower

Ask adults to help you use a knife or ask them to do this part.

Ingredients
1 red radish

1. Slice off the root end of the radish (see photo 1 and 2).
2. Make three thin cuts, spacing them evenly around radish (see photo 3 and 4).
3. Make three more thin cuts behind each first cut, making sure that the cuts meet near the bottom of the radish. Do not cut all the way through (see photo 5).
4. Holding bottom of radish, gently pull out the centre portion (see photo 6).
5. Place egg mimosa (sieved, hard-boiled egg yolk) in middle of the flower to create the pistil of the flower.

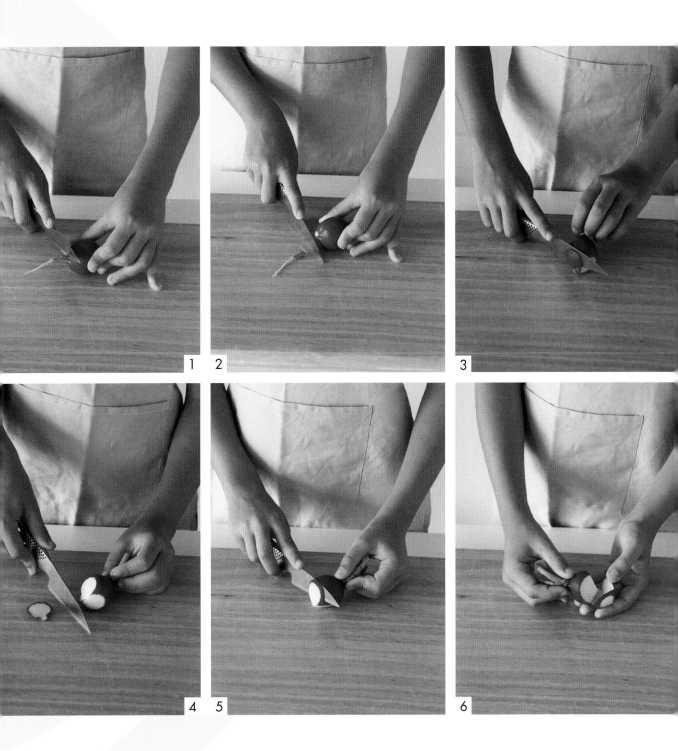

1 2 3
4 5 6

45
Garnishes and decorations

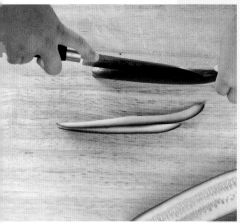

Preparing Fillings for Nori Rolls

When making nori rolls, one or more of the following fillings can be used. The preparation is always the same.

Vegetables for Thin Rolls

- Lebanese cucumber: cut lengthways, seeded and cut into long thin sticks (see photos opposite).
- Carrot: peeled and cut lengthways into strips and cooked with a small amount of sugar until just tender. Carrots strips may also be used raw.

Sweetened Cooked Carrot

Makes enough for 1 roll of sushi

Ingredients
1 small carrot
1 teaspoon superfine (caster) sugar
½ cup water

Utensils
knife, saucepan

1. Peel and cut the carrot into lengthways strips and cook in a saucepan with the sugar and water for 5 minutes over a low heat.
2. Set aside to cool down.

- Asparagus, French beans, snow peas: blanched.
- Avocados: cut lengthways into six equal strips.
- Tomatoes: cut in half, seeded and sliced into thin segments.
- Scallions (spring onions): the bottom portion trimmed and sliced lengthways.
- English spinach: blanched and cooled.
- Green salad leaves: rinsed and drained well.
- Bell peppers (capsicum): red or yellow, core and white veins removed. Cut into narrow strips.

Meat, Egg and Other Fillings

- Egg omelette strips (see Square Omelette or Thin Omelette recipes)
- Crab meat: sliced, broken into appropriate-sized sticks. Imitation crab meat or seafood sticks may also be used.
- Pickled daikon: cut into sticks.
- Sliced fresh tuna: It should be sashimi-quality and very fresh. Otherwise, it should be cooked.
- Canned tuna: well-drained, mixed with mayonnaise or miso.
- Salmon: fresh, smoked or canned, well drained.
- Jumbo shrimp (king prawns): cooked or tempura (see Fish and Seafood in Introduction)
- Grilled eel: Purchase pre-cooked grilled eel and slice it.
- Chicken, teriyaki chicken and deep-fried chicken: cut into strips. Other varieties such as tandoori chicken can also be used (see recipes for Teriyaki Sauce and *Tatsuta-age* (Savoury Deep-fried Chicken)).
- Beef: Thinly sliced beef, available from Asian butchers or grocery shops, braised in teriyaki sauce (see recipe for Teriyaki Sauce).
- Pork: lean pork steaks, sliced and then stir-fried in teriyaki sauce.
- Cheese strips: choose your favourite cheese
- Ham strips: choose your favourite ham
- Sausages: choose your favourite sausages and cook, then slice into smaller portions.

Paste and Sprinkles

- Umeboshi (pickled plum) paste
- sesame seeds
- furikake

Soy Sauce-flavoured Canned Tuna

These days you can find a huge variety of canned tuna in the shops. You can choose your preferred type or maybe you'd like to add a little zest with soy sauce.

Ingredients
1 small can tuna* (approximately 3½oz/95g in a can) in brine
1 teaspoon soy sauce
1–2 teaspoons superfine (caster) sugar

Utensils
saucepan, wooden spoon

*Instead of tuna, you could use a can of salmon.

1. Lightly squeeze the liquid out of the canned tuna.
2. Place tuna, soy sauce and sugar in a saucepan.
3. Cook over a low heat for about 5 minutes, stirring constantly. Remove from heat and allow to cool.

Grilled Salmon Flakes

Ingredients
pinch of salt
3½oz (100g) salmon fillet

Utensils
broiler/griller or oven

1. Sprinkle salt over salmon and leave for 10 minutes.
2. Place under the broiler/griller until cooked on one side. Turn and cook other side.
3. Allow to cool. Using your hands, break up salmon into flakes.

Avocado Tuna

Ingredients

¼ avocado, peeled and seed removed
1½oz (40g) canned tuna
pinch of salt
1 teaspoon white sesame seeds
½ teaspoon lemon juice

Utensils

bowl, fork

1. Mix all the ingredients in a bowl with a fork.

Minced Chicken in Soy Sauce

Ingredients

3½oz (100g) minced chicken
1 tablespoon mirin
1 tablespoon soy sauce
1 teaspoon superfine (caster) sugar
1 teaspoon water

Utensils

saucepan, cooking chopsticks or wooden spoon

1. Combine all ingredients in a saucepan over a low heat.
2. Stir with chopsticks until the mince has cooked through and turned brown.

Square Omelette
makes 3 strips for rolls

Ingredients
3 x 2oz (60g) eggs
pinch of salt
1 teaspoon soy sauce
2 tablespoons dashi
1 teaspoon superfine (caster)
  sugar
1 tablespoon oil, soaked onto a
  piece of kitchen paper

Utensils
bowl, fork or chopsticks, ,
  rectangular omelette pan
  (common size is about 5½–6
  x 7–7½in/14-15 x 18–19cm)
  or frying pan, a spatula

1. Break eggs into a bowl and beat with a fork or chopsticks.
2. Add salt, soy sauce, dashi and sugar and stir well.
3. This next step uses heat, so you may need to ask an adult to help. Spread the oiled kitchen paper over the surface and heat up over moderate heat.
4. Gently pour in a third of the mixture to cover base of omelette pan. Use a spatula to press out any air bubbles. When omelette sets and becomes dry, run a spatula around it to loosen (see photo 1).
5. With spatula or chopsticks, fold one-third of omelette from far side toward centre, then fold this over onto the remaining portion closest to you (see photo 2)
6. Using the oiled kitchen paper, ask an adult to wipe over the empty section of the pan, slide first omelette portion to the other end of the pan and pour in another third of mixture, lifting cooked omelette up to let it flow underneath (see photo 3 and 4).
7. When firm, fold the thicker portion over towards you as before, making a thick flat roll (see photo 5).
8. Continue adding mixture, cooking until firm and folding to make a triple-layered omelette (see photo 6).
9. Remove from heat. Turn omelette onto a plate to cool it down.
10. For nori roll fillings, slice into strips.
11. For nigiri-zushi cut into pieces 1in (2.5cm) wide and 2½in (7cm) long.
12. The omelette can also be eaten on its own, as tamagoyaki, cut into cubes.

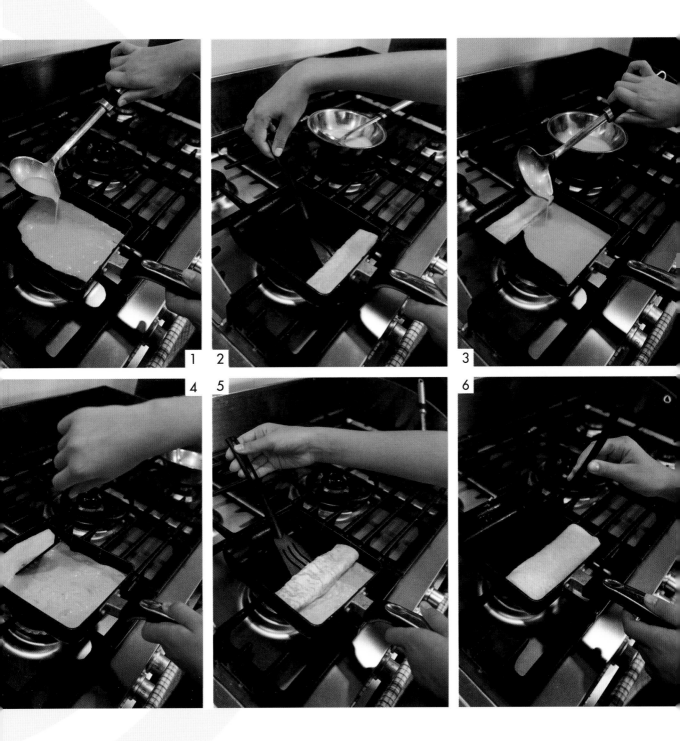

1 2 3
4 5 6

Thin Omelette
makes 1–2 sheets of omelette

This thin omelette can be used as a wrapper (for fukasa) or as a shredded decoration for sushi, such as chirashi-zushi.

Ingredients
1 egg
pinch of salt
*1 teaspoon potato starch mixed
    with 1 teaspoon water*
*1 tablespoon oil, to soak a
    piece of kitchen paper in a
    small bowl*

Utensils
*bowl, omelette pan or frying
    pan, spatula, bamboo stick,
    dry chopping board*

1. Break egg into a bowl and beat with salt and potato starch mixture.
2. Heat a pan over moderate heat and using chopsticks or tongs, wipe oiled kitchen paper over the pan.
3. Pour ½ egg mixture into pan and spread evenly by gently moving the pan.
4. When the edges become dry, place a bamboo stick lightly across the middle of the omelette then with a spatula fold the omelette over the stick. Using the stick, lift the thin omelette, turn it over and cook the other side for a few seconds. Transfer onto a chopping board or plate.
5. Repeat with remaining mixture.
6. When cooled down, lightly roll and thinly slice.

Teriyaki Sauce
makes about 1 cup

Teriyaki sauce is also available from Japanese or Asian groceries or major supermarkets, but you can make your own.

Ingredients
4 tablespoons superfine (caster) sugar or raw sugar
4 tablespoons soy sauce
4 tablespoons mirin
Optional: 1 teaspoon fresh ginger juice (made by grating fresh ginger and
    squeezing over a bowl)

Utensils
small saucepan

1. To make teriyaki sauce, combine all the ingredients in a saucepan and bring to the boil. Reduce heat and simmer for 3 minutes.

 # Teriyaki Chicken

Ingredients
A few drops of vegetable oil
7oz (200g) chicken thigh or breast*
1 cup teriyaki sauce (see recipe)

Utensils
frying pan, tongs or chopsticks

1. Drop a little oil onto the base of the frying pan and swirl to coat.
2. Heat the pan over a medium-high heat and add the chicken.
3. Fry over moderate heat until browned on each side.
4. Add teriyaki sauce and cook over low heat until cooked through.
5. Once it is cooled down, slice into bite-sized pieces.
*Beef, salmon or tuna can be used instead of chicken.

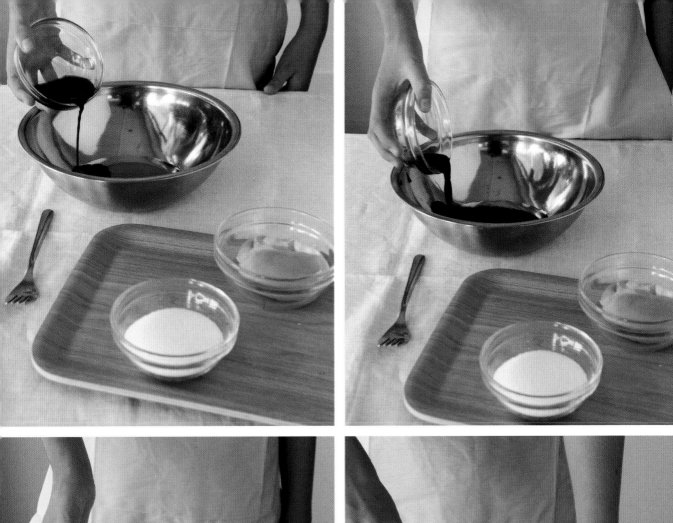

Tandoori Chicken

This tasty chicken can be sliced, chopped finely or cut into sticks for various recipes.

Ingredients

17½oz (500g) chicken breast fillet
½ teaspoon salt
1 tablespoon curry powder or tandoori paste
1 cup plain yoghurt
½ teaspoon ginger powder or fresh ginger (grated)
½ teaspoon grated garlic
1 tablespoon tomato paste

Utensils

bowl, fork, baking paper, baking tray, *oven

1. Place chicken in a bowl. With a fork, spear the chicken and rub it all over with salt.
2. Cover the chicken with all the ingredients and rub in with your hands. Refrigerate overnight or for half a day.
3. Preheat oven 400°F (200°C). Lay the baking paper on the tray. Remove some of the excess mixture from the chicken, and place chicken on the tray.
4. Bake in the oven for about 10–15 minutes or until cooked.

*You may also cook in a frying pan or griller.

Preparing fillings

Deep-frying

Before deep-frying

Cooking with oil, especially deep-frying, needs more care than other cooking, as the temperature of oil rises to more than 300°F (150°C). Deep-frying is not suitable for children. I recommend an adult cooks any food that requires deep-frying.

Safety tips for deep-frying:

1. Overheated oil can ignite. If the oil is allowed to become too hot, it will burst into flame. In case of an oil fire, NEVER USE WATER. Cover with a kitchen fire blanket or a lid if possible. Make sure to turn off the heat.
2. Oil and water do not mix. When cooking, keep water away from the hot oil. If water drops onto the heated oil, hot oil will splash out. This can cause burns. That is why you need to remove any excess water from foods before frying to prevent the oil from splattering. Letting ingredients sit on paper towels or coating them in flour, batter or breadcrumbs is also effective.
3. Preferably use a deep-fryer or a large saucepan or wok.
4. Add oil to the cold pan, leaving some space at the top, at least 4in (10cm), which allows a safety margin as oil bubbles up.
5. Heat the oil over medium heat. If you have a deep-frying thermometer, use it to measure when the oil is 350°F (180°C). If not, drop a few breadcrumbs into the oil, and when they quickly float up, the oil is ready.
6. Do not overcrowd in the pan when deep-frying. Leave a bit of space around each of the ingredients to cook evenly.
7. When removing food from the oil, always use a pair of tongs or a mesh ladle.

1

2

Shrimp (Prawn) Tempura

Ingredients
4 green jumbo shrimp (king prawns)
1 tablespoon potato starch
tempura batter

Note: Tempura batter is available from Japanese or Asian grocery shops and should be made according to the instructions on the packet. The batter can also be made by mixing ½ cup tempura mix flour with ½ cup refrigerated cold water. If you are unable to obtain tempura flour, make a batter using½ cup all-purpose (plain) flour, ½ beaten egg and ½ cup cold water.

Utensils
bowl, bamboo skewers, kitchen paper, plate, long-handled tongs, deep-fryer, pan or wok

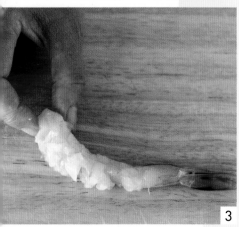

3

4

1. To prepare shrimp, first remove the head. Without cutting off the tail, remove the shell (see photo 1).
2. Use a bamboo stick to remove the vein from the back. Repeat with other 3 shrimp. Rinse and pat with kitchen paper.
3. Place the shrimp with its belly facing up on a chopping board. With a small knife, make 4 deep scores to prevent curling. After cutting, bend the shrimp in the opposite direction to its natural curve to further straighten it (see photos 2 and 3).
4. Pat with kitchen paper to dry. Coat shrimp with potato starch on a plate.
5. To make tempura batter, place flour in a bowl. Add refrigerated cold water. Using a fork or pair of chopsticks, roughly combine. Do not mix too much as it will become too starchy. It is ok if there are still a few lumps in the mixture. Keep the mixture in the refrigerator (see photo 4).
6. Ask an adult to help with this step. Put the oil in a deep-fryer, pan or wok and heat the oil to 350°F (180°C). To check the temperature, drop a small amount of the tempura batter into the oil, and when it quickly floats up, it is ready.

Holding one shrimp with tongs, carefully lower it into the oil, sweeping it across the oil as you lower it. Add each prawn in the same way. Turn each shrimp over when it becomes a light golden colour, and remove when cooked on both sides. Drain on a rack or kitchen paper on a plate.

Shrimp (Prawns) in Breadcrumbs

Note: Deep-frying is not suitable for children. I recommend an adult does the deep-frying steps.

Ingredients
4 green jumbo shrimp (king prawns)
2 tablespoons all-purpose (plain) flour
1 cup panko breadcrumbs or breadcrumbs
1 egg, beaten

Utensils
bamboo stick, kitchen paper, chopping board, bowl, plates, small knife, tongs

1. Prepare shrimp according to shrimp tempura recipe.
2. Put flour on a plate, beaten egg in a bowl or soup plate and breadcrumbs on a plate. Arrange plates in a line for easy dipping.
3. Holding one shrimp by the tail, coat shrimp with flour.
4. Dip the coated shrimp in the beaten egg.
5. Transfer onto the breadcrumbs and coat it evenly, pressing firmly with the fingers.
6. Repeat with other 3 shrimp.
7. Ask an adult to help with this step. Prepare the oil in a deep-frying pan and heat to 350°F (180°C).
8. Deep-fry shrimp until golden brown.
9. With tongs or a mesh ladle, transfer onto a rack or kitchen paper, to allow excess oil to drain.

Panko breadcrumbs are available from Japanese or Asian grocery shops.

Tatsuta-age (Savoury Deep-fried Chicken)

Note: Deep-frying is not suitable for children. I recommend an adult does the deep-frying part. Read the start of this section before cooking.

Makes about 6 pieces

Ingredients

7oz (200g) chicken thigh or breast
2-3 tablespoons potato starch, for dusting
vegetable oil, for deep-frying

Marinade

2 tablespoons soy sauce
1 tablespoon honey or sugar
Optional: 1 teaspoon crushed garlic and 1 teaspoon grated ginger, added to the marinade

Utensils

knife, small jug or cup, bowl or resealable plastic sandwich bag, kitchen paper, deep-fryer or deep frying pan (wok), tongs, plate or tray

1. Cut chicken into cubes, each piece about 1oz (30-35g).
2. Combine all the ingredients of marinade in a jug or cup and stir.
3. Place chicken in a plastic bag.
4. Add the marinade sauce into the bag.
5. Close the bag and massage chicken over the bag.
6. Put in refrigerator for at least 30 minutes.
7. Take out chicken from the bag and pat with kitchen paper.
8. Put potato starch on a plate and coat the chicken.
9. Heat up the oil to about 350°F (180°C). To check the temperature, drop in a small piece of bread and if it comes up to the surface quickly, it is ready. Deep-fry chicken cubes for 1 minute, take out and set aside for 1 minute on a tray or rack to steam. During this rest time, you can deep-fry another piece.
10. Deep-fry the rested chicken again for two minutes and drain well on a rack or kitchen paper.

Tonkatsu (Japanese-style Fried Pork)

Note: Deep-frying is not suitable for children. I recommend an adult does the deep-frying part. Read the start of this section before cooking.

Ingredients

1 piece pork loin (approximately 5oz/150g)
salt to taste
black pepper to taste
1 tablespoon all-purpose (plain) flour
2-3 tablespoons panko breadcrumbs or fine breadcrumbs
1 egg
vegetable oil for deep-frying

Utensils

two plates, small bowl for egg, deep-fryer or deep frying pan (such as wok), kitchen paper

1. Sprinkle the pork with salt and pepper.
2. Prepare flour and breadcrumbs on separate plates. Break egg into a bowl and beat it with a fork. Arrange flour, egg and breadcrumbs in a row.
3. Using your hands, transfer the pork onto the flour and coat with flour. Slightly pat off excess flour.
4. Dip the pork into the egg to coat. If you do not coat it with egg thoroughly, breadcrumbs will not attach.
5. Place pork onto the breadcrumbs and coat on both sides, pressing firmly with your hands.
6. Heat the oil to about 350°F (180°C).
7. Deep-fry pork until golden brown. During this, turn over a couple of times. Drain well over a rack or kitchen paper.
8. Once it has cooled down, cut into required size.

Tip: For sushi roll, before deep-frying, you can also create pork sticks by cutting the pork loin into strips and coating, then deep-frying.

Dressings

You can use your favourite brands of mayonnaise. Japanese mayonnaise contains more egg yolk than Western varieties and is generally not as sweet.

Kiwi Fruit Mayonnaise
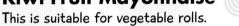
This is suitable for vegetable rolls.

makes ½ cup

Ingredients
½ kiwi fruit, flesh scooped out
2 tablespoons mayonnaise

Utensils
potato masher or fork, bowl

1. Place all kiwi fruit and mayonnaise in a bowl and mash with a potato masher or fork.

Lemon Jelly

Ingredients
3 tablespoons lemon juice
1 tablespoon superfine (caster) sugar
1 tablespoon water
1 teaspoon gelatine, soaked in a teaspoon water
a pinch of lemon zest

Utensils
saucepan, spoon, fork, bowl

Tip

Use a cheese grater or lemon zester to make zest. Instead of lemon, fresh ginger can be used with this recipe.

1. Combine lemon juice, sugar and water in a saucepan. Over low heat, bring it to the boil.
2. Add gelatine and cook until dissolved, stirring with a spoon.
3. Remove from the heat and transfer into a bowl.
4. Cool it down and refrigerate until set.
5. Break up into small pieces with a fork.

Sweet Soy Sauce Mayonnaise

Ingredients
¼ teaspoon soy sauce
¼ teaspoon raw sugar or superfine (caster) sugar
2 tablespoons Japanese mayonnaise

Utensils
heatproof bowl

1. Put soy sauce and sugar in a heatproof bowl.
2. Heat in microwave oven for 5 seconds in high heat. Mix until sugar is dissolved.
3. Once it has cooled down, add mayonnaise and mix well.

Soy Sauce Jelly

Ingredients
1 teaspoon gelatine powder
1 teaspoon water
¼ cup dashi stock
2 tablespoons soy sauce
½ teaspoon superfine (caster) sugar

Utensils
small saucer, small saucepan, spoon, fork

1. Soak gelatine with 1 teaspoon water in a small saucer and leave for 5 minutes.
2. Add dashi, soy sauce and gelatine in a small saucepan (see photo 1).
3. Over low heat, cook, stirring with a spoon, until dissolved.
4. Remove from the heat and transfer the gelatine mixture into a bowl or container.
5. Refrigerate until set.
6. With a fork, roughly scramble jelly (see photos 2, 3 and 4).

Wasabi Mayonnaise
Wasabi is as hot as English mustard. You might like how hot it is; however, you can control the hotness by the amount of wasabi powder/paste you use. Ask an adult to taste it first.

Ingredients
2 tablespoons mayonnaise
1 teaspoon wasabi paste or less for milder taste

1. Mix all the ingredients in bowl until combined.

Let's Make Sushi!

Nori-maki

Nori-maki rolls are the most popular type of sushi. There are many varieties, both thin and thick, ones with nori on the outside or nori on the inside. The thin rolls usually have Japanese names, such as *kappa-maki*, or *kampyō-maki* and the thick ones may have American names, like California rolls (inside-out rolls), Boston rolls (with grilled salmon skin), Philadelphia rolls (with cream cheese), spider rolls (with soft-shelled crab tempura).

Before you start, you need to prepare some sushi rice (see Essential Ingredients for Sushi in Introduction) and fillings (see Basic Techniques).

Things to know before making sushi rolls:
- Place the bamboo sushi mat on a cutting board with the loose strings furthest away from you. If the bamboo sticks of the mat are flat on one side, place that side up.
- Arrange nori, fillings and rice close around the board.
- Make sure you have a bowl of vinegar water, called 'tezu' (1 teaspoon rice vinegar in 1 cup water) handy, for wetting your hands when you handle the rice.
- Place a sheet of nori on the bamboo mat, smooth side down, so that the length is parallel to the bamboo sticks and stand in front of the bamboo mat.
- Some people encase their bamboo mats in plastic wrap. This makes it both easier to work with and easier to clean, especially for beginners. I prefer to use a bamboo mat without plastic—I like to feel the natural texture of the mat.

Roll 1 — Mini Roll

Ingredients
1 sheet of one-quarter size nori (square)
1 tablespoon sushi rice
1 strip of filling

Utensils
mini bamboo sushi mat (approximately 5 x 7in/13 x 18cm)
a bowl of tezu

makes 1 mini-roll

Especially for small kids, this mini roll is good for little hands to start with. Cut a whole nori sheet into quarters and use one quarter.

1. Place nori on a sushi mat, rough side facing you (see photo 1).
2. Place a tablespoon of sushi rice on front left side of nori (see photos 2 and 3).
3. Spread rice over nori with a spoon or moistened fingers, leaving one-third of the space free from rice on the nori (see photos 4 and 5).
4. Place a filling on the centre of the rice.
5. Hold the mat with your thumbs and index fingers and roll while pushing filling with fingers up to the end of rice (see photo 6).
6. Lift up top of the mat and roll to close up the nori.
7. You can eat straight away or you may slice in half or into 3 pieces. For small children, use a petite knife instead of a chef's knife.

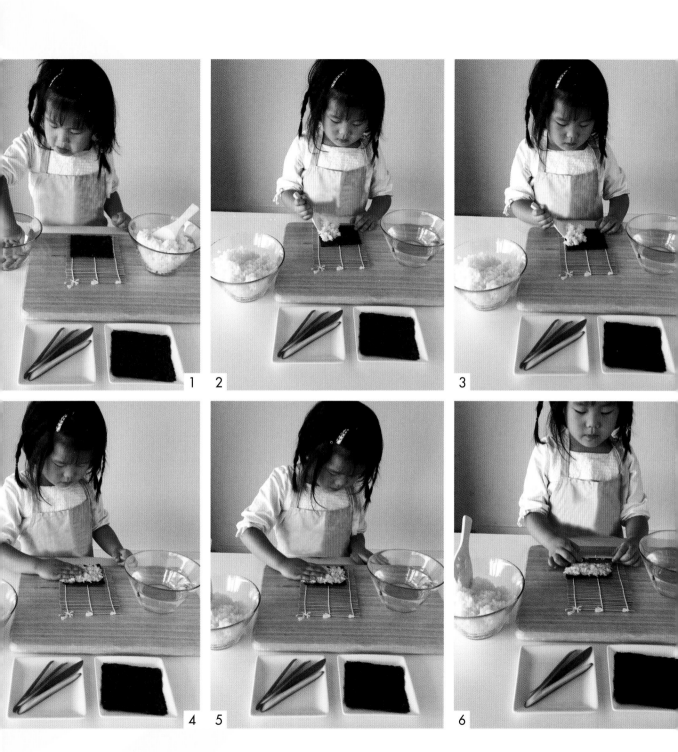

1   2   3

4   5   6

Nori-maki

California Mini Roll

Ingredients

*5–5½oz (150–160g) sushi rice
    or pink sushi rice*
1 nori sheet
*1 strip sweetened cooked carrot
    (see recipe in Preparing
    Fillings for Nori Rolls)*
*1 strip cucumber (see Preparing
    Fillings for Nori Rolls)*
1 cheddar cheese stick
1 slice ham, of your choice
soy sauce for serving

Utensils

*scissors, mini sushi mat,
    sheet of plastic wrap, tezu
    (vinegar water) in small bowl,
    chopping board, knife*

makes 4 mini rolls

1. Fold nori into quarters to make 4 square sheets and cut with scissors.
2. Cover a sushi mat with a sheet of plastic wrap, folding it over the edges to attach it to the back of mat.
3. Place a square nori on a sushi mat.
4. Dip right fingers in tezu.
5. With moistened fingers, spread rice over the nori square, covering the entire sheet.
6. Carefully pick up rice-covered nori by the corners and quickly turn it over and place upside down on the mat.
7. Arrange fillings along centre of nori.
8. Roll rice and nori on the mat, pressing in on ingredients with your fingertips, stopping 2cm (¾in) short of the end.
9. Lift up mat, roll back a little, then roll forward to join the edges.
10. Use gentle pressure to shape, either round, oval or square.
11. Transfer the roll onto a dry board and with a knife and cut each roll in half.
12. Arrange sushi on a plate.

Roll 2 — Hoso-maki (Thin Roll)

Ingredients

2½oz (80g) sushi rice
1 half nori sheet
1–2 fillings (see Basic
*   Techniques — Preparing*
*   Fillings for Nori Rolls), such*
*   as cucumber sticks*

Utensils

bamboo sushi mat, tezu
(bowl of vinegar water), knife,
chopping board, damp towel

makes 1 thin roll or 8 or 6 pieces

For right-handers

1. Arrange ingredients and a sushi mat in front of you.
2. Place nori on the mat, rough side facing to you.
3. Place rice on the front left-hand corner.
4. Dip the tips of your right fingers into tezu to moisten them and start spreading rice evenly. Do not cover the whole nori sheet. Leave one-quarter of nori, about ¾in (2cm), on far side uncovered.
5. Place filling along centre of rice, covering the entire length.
6. Lift up the edge of the sushi mat closest to you with your thumbs and index fingers, placing your other fingers over the filling to hold them in place. Roll the rice and nori around the filling. The rice-free portion of nori should still be visible.
7. Lift up the top of the mat and roll the entire roll.
8. Making sure the closed side of the roll is on the bottom, gently but firmly shape the sushi in the mat to form a cylindrical shape, pressing gently with tips of fingers along the sides of the roll, not the top.
9. Moisten your fingers with tezu and flatten each end.
10. Unroll the mat and move the roll to a dry board.
11. Ask an adult to help you slice the sushi. To slice the sushi you will need a chef's knife, chopping board and damp kitchen towel or cloth.
12. Place the roll on the dry chopping board. Moisten the knife with the damp towel and cut roll in half, then cut each half in half again. Then cut each quarter in half to make 8 equal-sized pieces in total.
13. Or slice roll in half, then cut both rolls twice to give 6 equal-sized pieces.

Let's Make Sushi!

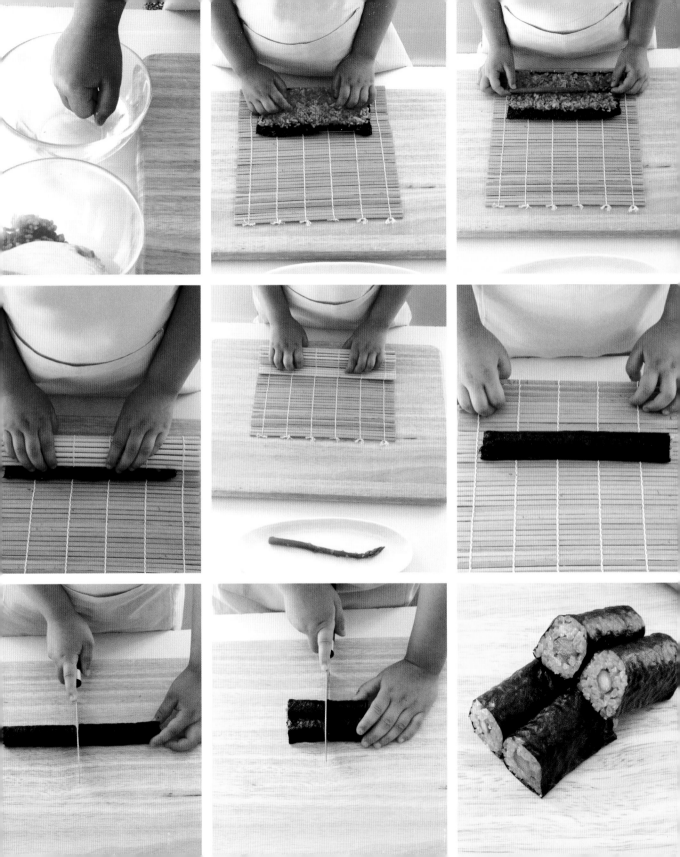

Avocado Tuna Roll

Ingredients

1½oz (40g) canned tuna
¼ small avocado
½ teaspoon lemon juice
pinch of salt
½ nori sheet
2½oz (80g) sushi rice

Utensils

fork, small bowl, bamboo sushi mat, chopping board, tezu (a bowl of water or vinegar water)

makes 1 thin roll, 6 pieces

1. Mash tuna and avocado with a fork in a bowl.
2. Add lemon juice and a pinch of salt and combine.
3. Place nori on sushi mat.
4. Put sushi rice on the front left corner and with moistened fingers spread rice over nori sheet, leaving 1cm (1/3in) of bare nori at far end.
5. Arrange avocado and tuna in a line along the centre.
6. Roll mat over once, away from you, pressing ingredients in to keep roll firm, up to the rice free part.
7. With the mat still covering nori, but not the rice free portion of nori, hold rolling mat in position and press all round to make roll firm with fingers.
8. Lift up top of mat and roll over a little bit more to seal the joins.
9. With mat still in place, roll once more, and use fingertip pressure to shape roll in cylindrical form.
10. Remove mat and place roll on a chopping board and slice.

Ebi-roll (Shrimp/Prawn Roll)

Ingredients

1 tablespoon mayonnaise
1/4 teaspoon curry powder
1/2 sheet nori
2 1/2oz (80g) sushi rice
2 jumbo shrimp (king prawn)
    tempura
few small salad leaves

Utensils

small bowl, bamboo sushi mat,
    chopping board, tezu (bowl
    of water or vinegar water)

makes 1 roll, 6 pieces

1. Mix mayonnaise and curry powder in a small bowl.
2. Place nori on sushi mat.
3. Put sushi rice on the front left corner and with moistened fingers spread rice over nori sheet, leaving 1cm (1/3in) of bare nori at far end (see photo 1).
4. Spread mayonnaise mixture on top (see photo 2).
5. Arrange salad leaves on top of king prawns (see photo 3).
6. Arrange king prawns along centre with tails poking out from each end of nori (see photos 4 and 5).
7. Roll mat over once, away from you, pressing ingredients in to keep roll firm, up to the rice-free part.
8. With the mat still covering nori, but not the rice free portion of nori, hold rolling mat in position and press all round to make roll firm with fingers.
9. Lift up top of mat and roll over a little bit more to seal the joins (see photo 6).
10. With mat still in place, roll once more, and use fingertip pressure to shape roll in cylindrical form.
11. Remove mat and place roll on a chopping board and slice.

Sweet Soy Sauce-flavoured Beef Roll

Ingredients

drop of vegetable oil

*1oz (30g) thinly sliced beef
(available from Japanese
grocery shops in the frozen
section, or some Asian
butchers)*

*1 teaspoon superfine (caster)
sugar*

1 teaspoon soy sauce

few small salad leaves

½ sheet nori

4oz (120g) sushi rice

Utensils

*frying pan, bamboo sushi mat,
small bowl, tezu (bowl of
water or vinegar water)*

makes 1 roll, 6 pieces

1. Put oil in a frying pan and heat it up.
2. Add beef, sugar and soy sauce and stir until it is cooked through.
3. Remove from the heat and set aside.
4. Place nori on sushi mat.
5. Put sushi rice on the front left corner and with moistened fingers spread rice over nori sheet, leaving $1/3$in (1cm) of bare nori at far end.
6. Arrange beef and salad leaves in a line.
7. Roll mat over once, away from you, pressing ingredients in to keep roll firm, up to the rice-free part.
8. With the mat still covering nori, but not the rice-free portion of nori, hold rolling mat in position and press all round to make roll firm with fingers.
9. Lift up top of mat and roll over a little bit more to seal the joins.
10. With mat still in place, roll once more, and use fingertip pressure to shape roll in cylindrical form.
11. Remove mat and place roll on a chopping board and slice.

Wisteria Sushi

Ingredients

6oz (180g) sushi rice
½ teaspoon yukari (dried shiso)
½ teaspoon roasted white
   sesame seeds
1 sheet nori, cut in half
gari (pickled ginger), for serving
   on the side

Utensils

2 bowls, 2 spoons, tezu (bowl
   of water), bamboo sushi mat,
   chopping board, chef's knife

makes 2 rolls (16 pieces)

1. Divide sushi rice and put into two bowls.
2. Add yukari to one bowl and sesame to the other bowl, and using moistened spoons, combine with the sushi rice.
3. Lay one half of the nori sheet lengthways on sushi mat, shiny side down.
4. Dip tip of your right fingers into tezu to moisten them and spread yukari rice evenly. Do not cover the whole nori sheet. Leave a quarter of the nori, about ¾in (2cm), on far side uncovered.
5. Lift up the edge of the sushi mat closest to you with your thumbs and index fingers, placing your other fingers over the filling to hold them in place, roll the rice and nori over the filling. The rice-free portion of nori should still be visible.
6. Lift up the top of mat and roll the entire roll.
7. Unroll mat. Gently press edges together to form a teardrop-shape.
8. Moisten your fingers with tezu and flatten each end of the roll.
9. Unroll the mat and move the roll to a dry board.
10. For slicing, place the roll on a dry chopping board. Wipe a knife with a dampened kitchen towel. Slice roll in half, and then cut each half into four equal-sized pieces.
11. Repeat using sesame rice.
12. Arrange in two rows (like the photo opposite) next to each other on a plate to resemble a spray of wisteria.

Roll 3 — Chu-maki (Mid-size Roll)

Ingredients
1 nori sheet
4½oz (130g) sushi rice
2–3 fillings of your choice (see Basic Techniques – Preparing Fillings for Nori Rolls)

Utensils
bamboo sushi mat, chopping board, knife, tezu (bowl of vinegar water)

makes 1 roll or 8 pieces

This is a roll that takes less effort. The size makes it good for school lunchbox.

1. Place whole nori on the sushi mat.
2. Place rice on the middle of the left-hand side of nori sheet. Leave rice-free space on both sides.
3. Moisten fingers in the tezu and spread rice evenly across nori, leaving ¾in (2cm) strips at front and back.
4. Place filling on the centre and roll same as thin roll.
5. With a moistened knife, slice the roll in half and then into 6–8 pieces.

Roll 4 — Futo-maki (Thick Roll)

Ingredients

1 nori sheet
5oz (150g) sushi rice
1 teaspoon furikake or tobiko
3-4 fillings of your choice (see Basic Techniques — Preparing Fillings for Nori Rolls)

Utensils

bamboo sushi mat, tezu (bowl of vinegar water)

makes 1 roll or 8 pieces

1. Place nori on sushi mat (see photo 1).
2. Put sushi rice on the front left corner, moisten your fingers and spread rice over nori sheet, leaving ¾in (2cm) of bare nori at far end.
3. Sprinkle furikake or spoon tobiko along centre of rice using back of a spoon to spread (see photo 2).
4. Arrange filling along centre (see photo 3).
5. Roll mat over once, away from you, pressing ingredients in to keep roll firm, leaving ¾in (2cm) of nori rice-free (see photo 4).
6. With the mat still covering the roll, but not the rice-free portion of nori, hold rolling mat in position and press all round to make roll firm with fingers (see photo 5).
7. Lift up top of mat and roll over a little bit more to seal the joints.
8. With mat still in place, roll once more, and use fingertip pressure to shape roll in a cylindrical form.
9. To slice the roll, you will need a chef's knife, chopping board and damp kitchen towel or cloth (see photo 6).
10. Place the roll on the dry chopping board. Moisten the knife with damp towel and cut roll in half, then cut each half in half again. Then cut each quarter in half to make 8 equal-sized pieces in total.

1 2 3

4 5 6

93
Nori-maki

Roll 5 — Uramaki (Inside-out/ California Roll)

Ingredients

½ cup sushi rice

½ nori sheet

2 teaspoons sesame seeds on a plate

3–4 fillings of your choice (see Basic Techniques – Preparing Fillings for Nori Rolls)

Utensils

bamboo sushi mat, plastic wrap, tezu (a bowl of vinegar water)

makes ½ roll or 4 pieces

Inside-out rolls may look difficult, but they are actually easier to roll for the beginner than ordinary sushi rolls. Plastic wrap is used to keep the sushi rice from sticking to the bamboo mat. If the roll is not served straight away, it can be wrapped in plastic wrap to prevent it drying out. You can enjoy trying many different toppings for the outside of the sushi rice, such as flying fish roe, egg mimosa, furikake (sprinkles), sesame seeds or flaked green nori. You can also make mini inside-out rolls, using a quarter sheet of nori, and 1½ tablespoons rice on a small sushi mat.

1. Place nori sheet on mat (see photo 1).
2. Put rice on the front left corner of nori and then spread it out with moistened fingers, covering the entire nori sheet (see photos 2 and 3).
3. Cover the sushi rice and mat with a sheet of plastic wrap, folding it over the edges to attach it to back of mat. Or cut plastic wrap slightly larger than the mat and place over the nori and rice on the mat (see photo 4).
4. Insert one hand under the nori and carefully pick up rice-covered nori by corners, quickly turn it over and place upside down on the mat (see photos 5 and 6).
5. Arrange fillings along centre of nori (see photo 7)
6. Proceed to roll rice and nori on the mat, pressing in on ingredients with your fingertips, stopping ¾in (2cm) short of the end (see photo 8).
7. Lift up mat, roll back a little, then roll forward to join the edges. Use gentle pressure to shape, either round, oval, tear-drop shape or square (see photo 9).
8. Transfer the roll onto a dry board and with a chef's knife, cut each roll in half, then cut both in half again. Then cut four quarters in half to make 4 equal-sized pieces. Coat each piece with toppings, such as sesame seeds.

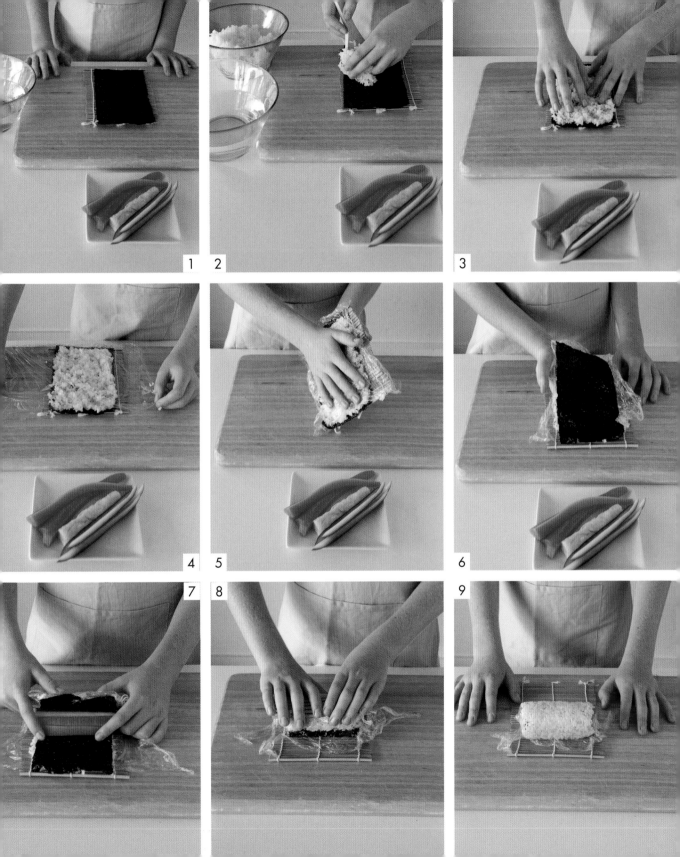

Tiger Roll

Ingredients

1 nori sheet
less than ½ cup sushi rice
1 tablespoon tobiko (flying fish roe)
1 tablespoon black roasted sesame seeds
3 fillings of your choice, such as beef teriyaki, green salad, carrot sticks (see Basic Techniques – Preparing Fillings for Nori Rolls)

makes 1 roll

1. Follow the same method as listed in the recipe for Roll 5—Uramaki, Inside-out Roll/California Roll.
2. After you have made the roll and sliced it, coat half the pieces with tobiko and the rest with black sesame seeds. Arrange in alternate colours, like tiger stripes, on a plate.

Dragon Roll

Ingredients
1 nori sheet
less than 1 cup sushi rice
2 cooked jumbo shrimp (king prawns)
4 avocado slices (see Basic Techniques – Preparing Fillings for Nori Rolls)
4 Lebanese cucumber sticks (see Basic Techniques – Preparing Fillings for Nori Rolls)
1 packet grilled eel, frozen or vacuum packed
1 tablespoon tobiko (flying fish roe)
2 carrot sticks for dragon's whiskers decoration

Utensils
bamboo stick, knife, chopping board, bamboo mat covered with plastic wrap, tezu (or bowl of water)

makes 1 roll or 8 pieces

1. Prepare eel by heating according to instructions on the pack. Allow to cool.
2. Cut eel lengthways into 3 strips ¼–½in (1-1.5cm) thick. Only 1 strip is required for this roll. You can use the other strips to make more dragon rolls, or as fillings for other rolls such as futo-maki.
3. To prepare the shrimp, remove head and shell from one shrimp, leaving the tail in place to use as the dragon's tail. Remove head, shell and tail from the other shrimp. With a bamboo stick, take out vein from the back of the shrimp.
4. Place bamboo mat on a dry area, and put nori on the mat. With moistened fingers spread rice all over the nori sheet, and flip it over so that the rice is now facing downwards and the nori is on top.
5. Arrange avocado and cucumber along centre of nori. Line up king prawns, making sure the prawn tail is sticking out the end, to be the dragon's tail.
6. Roll the dragon roll following the method for Roll 5, Uramaki, Inside-out Roll.
7. With the roll still on the bamboo mat, place the eel strip along the top of the roll and use the bamboo mat to secure it to the roll.
8. Transfer the roll onto a dry board. With a knife, cut roll in half, then cut each half into 4 equal-sized pieces to make 8 pieces, the last with the tail protruding.
9. Sprinkle tobiko on top alongside the eel strip. Transfer to a plate, positioning the rolls in the shape of a dragon using your imagination. Create dragon eyes with tobiko, and dragon whiskers with carrot sticks. If you like, you can use one of the shrimp heads to create a dramatic dragon's head.

Roll 6 — Tazuna-zushi (Rope Sushi/ Rainbow Roll)

Ingredients

about 6oz (170g) sushi rice

3 strips cucumber (see Basic Techniques — Preparing Fillings for Nori Rolls)

2 cooked jumbo shrimp (king prawns)

1 slice cheese or 2 thin egg omelette strips (cut into similar size as the cucumber strips, see Basic Techniques — Preparing Fillings for Nori Rolls)

other options: carrot, blanched snow peas

soy sauce to serve

Utensils

chopping board, petite knife (small knife) and chef's knife, bamboo sushi mat, chopsticks, 1 sheet plastic wrap (slightly larger than bamboo sushi mat), tezu (bowl of vinegar water)

makes 1 roll

Tazuna means 'twisted rope' so tazuna-zushi is a rope-shaped sushi. Choose three ingredients in different colours for toppings to make it look like a rainbow.

1. To prepare shrimp, peel each prawn and remove the head and tail. Place shrimp on a chopping board.
2. With a petite knife make a deep slit down the underside of each shrimp and spread open like a butterfly.
3. With a table knife or small knife slice cheese in half.
4. Place a chopstick horizontally slightly above the centre, on the plastic wrap placed on the bamboo mat (see photo 1).
5. Along the chopstick, arrange cucumber, shrimp and cheese alternately each piece just touching the next diagonally across the centre of the plastic wrap (see photo 2).
6. With moist hands, spread sushi rice evenly over the slices. Take away chopstick (see photo 3).
7. Hold the edge of the mat and fold in half. Push firmly with your hands to form a neat cylinder (see photos 4 and 5).
8. Unroll the mat and transfer the sushi to a dry board (see photo 6).
9. Remove the plastic wrap and cut each sushi roll widthways into half and then halve each piece (see photo 7).
10. Serve with soy sauce.

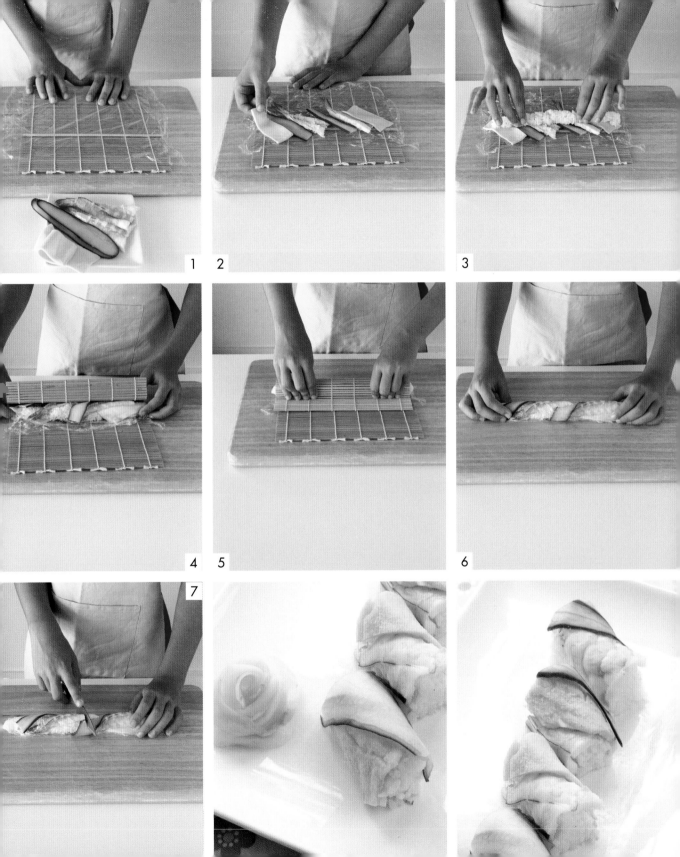

Mini Tazuna-zushi (Mini Rope/ Rainbow Roll)

Ingredients

2½oz (80g) sushi rice
2 cucumber strips (2in/5cm long)
1 carrot or ham stick
1 strip of cheese or thin egg omelette
soy sauce to serve

Utensils

small bamboo sushi mat, 1 sheet plastic wrap (slightly larger than bamboo sushi mat), tezu (bowl of vinegar water)

Using the same method as tazuna-zushi, except this is only a quarter of the size.

1. Prepare your ingredients following the method from the tazuna-zushi recipe.
2. Place a chopstick horizontally slightly above the centre.
3. Along the chopstick, arrange cucumber, carrot or ham, cheese or omelette, just touching the next diagonally across the centre of the plastic wrap.
4. With moist hands, spread sushi rice evenly over the slices.
5. Hold the edge of the mat and fold in half. Push firmly with your hands to form a neat cylinder.
6. Unroll the mat and transfer the sushi to a dry board.
7. Remove the plastic wrap and cut each sushi roll into half.
8. Serve with soy sauce.

Uzumaki Roll (Spiral Roll)

Ingredients

2 nori sheets, halved
3¼oz (110g) sushi rice or brown sushi rice
1½oz (40g) spreadable cream cheese
2–4 carrot sticks
2 cucumber sticks
2 cooked jumbo shrimp (king prawns), shells and tails removed or 1 slice ham

Utensils

sushi mat, knife, chopping board, tezu (water with vinegar), table knife

makes 12 pieces

1. Place a nori sheet lengthways on a sushi mat.
2. Dip your fingers into the tezu and with moistened fingers take the rice and spread it all over the nori.
3. With a table knife, spread cream cheese over the rice.
4. Top with one of the fillings—either carrot, cucumber or shrimp/ham horizontally in the centre of the nori roll.
5. Lift up the edge of the sushi mat closest to you and scroll the nori up to the end.
6. Form a round shape, pressing gently with tips of fingers over the mat.
7. Place the roll on a dry chopping board. Run a knife along a dampened kitchen towel.
8. Slice roll in half, then cut both rolls once again to make 4 pieces.

Onigiri-roll (Triangle Roll)

Ingredients
½ nori sheet
½ cup cooked rice or sushi rice
4 small ume-boshi (pickled plum), deseeded

Utensils
small sushi rolling mat

makes half-roll or 4 pieces

1. On a dry board, place nori lengthways on the sushi mat.
2. Spoon rice on the centre of the nori.
3. Place ume-boshi on the rice.
4. Roll up to make nori roll, then while still rolled in the mat, shape into a triangular shape.
5. Slice this to make 4 pieces.

Teardrop Roll in Flower Pattern

Ingredients
2½oz (80g) sushi rice
½ nori sheet
2 cucumber sticks (see Basic
    Techniques – Preparing
    Fillings for Nori Rolls)
1 hard-boiled quail egg, cherry
    tomato, strawberry or other
    attractive item for centre of
    flower

Utensils
bamboo sushi mat, tezu
    (or bowl of water), knife,
    chopping board

1. Roll sushi as per Roll 2 – Hoso-maki, Thin Roll (with cucumber). By pressing with your fingers on one side only along the length of the roll, you can make a wedge shape which produces attractive 'petals' when cut across the roll.
2. With a knife slice into 10 pieces.
3. Cut a quail egg lengthways.
4. Arrange rolls in a flower pattern with a halved quail egg or other decoration in centre.

Flower Roll

Ingredients
2 nori sheets
2oz (60g) sushi rice
5oz (150g) pink sushi rice
1 cheese stick or omelette

Utensils
scissors, bamboo sushi mat,
*   tezu (bowl of vinegar water),*
*   knife*

makes 4 pieces

Thin sticks of pink rice wrapped in nori, arranged round a cheese stick create beautiful sushi flowers when the roll is cut.

1. Fold nori sheets in half and cut with scissors. You will only need 3 of these pieces. Keep one half whole, and fold and cut the other two into 3 strips as per photo 1. Now you have 6 rectangular small nori sheets. You only use 5 pieces.
2. On a dry board, place a sushi mat and arrange one-sixth small nori sheet, one edge of the nori lining up with the front edge of the mat.
3. Dip your right fingers into the tezu. With damp fingers take about 1 tablespoonful sushi rice and spread evenly over two-thirds of the nori, leaving a space at the far edge.
4. Lift the front edge of the mat and roll up to the end of the rice.
5. Repeat steps 2 to 4 to make 4 more petal sticks. Set aside.
6. Arrange half size nori on sushi mat lengthways.
7. Spread rice evenly, leaving about 1in (3cm) at the far edge of nori.
8. On the sushi mat, lay 3 petal sticks and place cheese in centre and arrange the remaining two sticks around cheese.
9. Lift the front edge of the mat and roll up.
10. With a wet knife, slice the roll into 4 pieces.

Nori-maki

Snowman Roll

Ingredients

1 sheet nori
3½oz (100g) sushi rice
*4 cooked French beans
  (¼in/1cm long) or asparagus
  for hat*
*8 pieces black sesame for
  decoration*
*4 small triangle-shaped carrot
  pieces for nose*

Utensils

*scissors, tezu (water), bamboo
  sushi mat, knife, chopping
  board*

makes 4 pieces

1. Prepare nori. Fold nori sheet in half horizontally and, using scissors, cut in half.
2. Using one of them prepare head and body part. Fold one of the halved nori sheets in half again. The quarter nori sheet will be used as a body. Cut one-third of quartered sheet and use two-thirds of the sheet for head.
3. Place halved nori sheet on a bamboo mat lengthways.
4. To make a body part, place one quarter nori sheet on a mat or you may roll just with your hands.
5. Dip your fingers in water and put about one tablespoon sushi rice on the nori and spread it over leaving ⅔in (1.5cm) bare nori at far end. Roll up stopping ⅔in (1.5cm) short of the end and roll it entirely.
6. To make a head part, place two-thirds of quartered nori and spread rice, leaving ⅓in (1cm) bare at far end. Roll up with hands (see photos 2 and 3).
7. Now assemble together. Dip your fingers in water and put rice on the centre, and spread rice over nori sheet, leaving ¾in (2cm) bare nori at far end. Put the smaller nori roll as the head and the large nori roll as the body part. Place them both in the centre of the rice (see photos 4 and 5).
8. Arrange a French bean along the head part (see photo 5).
9. Roll mat over once, away from you, pressing fillings in to keep roll firm, leaving ¾in (2cm) of nori rice-free. Hold rolling mat in position, press all round to make roll firm with fingers. Lift up top of mat and roll over to seal the joints. Use fingertip pressure to shape roll.
10. Place the roll on a dry chopping board. Moisten a knife and slice it into quarters.
11. Arrange the pieces on a plate, and decorate with black sesame seeds for the eyes and carrots for the mouth.

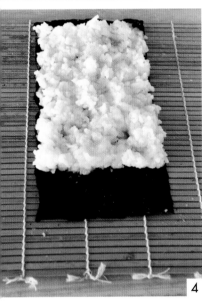

Nigiri-zushi

Nigiri-zushi literally means hand-moulded sushi, which is an oblong-shaped white sushi rice combined with toppings, usually slices of raw fish or other seafood. It looks very simple, but can be difficult to master, particularly with some of the delicate seafood toppings. It might be a good idea to get started with some simple toppings. Variations of nigiri-zushi are gunkan (battleship sushi) and temari-zushi (hand-ball sushi).

Gunkan (battleship sushi)

When making gunkan, remember that moistened hands are good for touching the sushi rice, but it is best to have dry hands when handling nori because nori is like paper and will shrivel up when wet. When you are making these sushi, prepare all the rice shapes first, leaving the wrapping until last, otherwise the nori will become wet and may break or go soggy.

Usually, the toppings are loose ingredients and in Japan, the most popular toppings are salmon roe (caviar), flying fish roe (tobikko), and chopped tuna. In this book, we have used canned tuna, corn, shredded steamed chicken and salad leaves, with soy sauce or mayonnaise. Soy sauce jelly, lemon jelly or beetroot jam can also be used for decoration (see Basic Techniques for recipes).

Toppings
- jumbo shrimp (king prawns) (see Fish and Seafood)
- grilled eel (see below)
- avocado (see below)
- salmon, fresh or smoked
- snow peas, cooked
- egg omelette, sliced
- ham, sliced
- cheese, sliced
- chicken teriyaki (see Teriyaki Chicken recipe), steamed or grilled chicken
- beef (see below)
- sausage, grilled and cut in half or sliced
- spam (popular in Hawaii and Korea), sliced and cooked

Nigiri-zushi in gunkan style (battleship)

- caviar
- sea urchin
- canned tuna
- canned salmon
- chicken, grilled and shredded
- fruits, such as blueberries

How to prepare toppings

Avocado

1. Place avocado lengthways on a board.
2. Hold avocado with one hand and with a medium-sized knife slice slowly cut down the centre lengthways around the seed, starting from the top end.
3. Hold avocado and twist clockwise with hands and rotate to separate two halves.
4. Slip a tablespoon in between the seed and fruit and gently remove the seed.
5. Cut into 4 pieces.
6. Peel the outer skin and slice.
7. If some of the darker parts remain on the fruit, you need to cut them away.

Beef

- Use sliced roast beef or thinly sliced beef in teriyaki flavour for your nigiri-zushi.

To make teriyaki beef, marinate 3½oz (100g) thinly sliced beef (available from Japanese grocers or Asian butchers) with 1 teaspoon teriyaki sauce (see recipe). Lightly stir fry.

Grilled eel

Warm up a pack of eel following the instruction on the packet. Transfer onto the board and slice (see Slicing Fish Fillets recipe).

Nigiri-zushi

Ingredients
5½oz (160g) sushi rice
8 pieces of toppings (select from variety of toppings list)
wasabi, if you like it hot
gari (pickled ginger), for garnish
soy sauce, for serving

Utensils
tezu (bowl of water or vinegar water), platter

makes 8 pieces

1. Prepare all of the toppings.
2. Moisten hand with the vinegar water and pick up about 1 tablespoonful rice. Form into a ball, pressing gently with the hand but do not squeeze tightly (see photos 1, 2 and 3).
3. Place one topping in the palm of your other hand. If you like wasabi, spread on a dab of wasabi with one finger.
4. Place rice on the topping and with index and middle fingers press firmly to form a mounded shape (see photo 4).
5. Roll sushi over and press again with two fingers against the topping (see photo 5 and 6).
6. Rotate sushi 360 degrees and press again with two fingers against the topping (see photos 7 and 8).
7. Arrange on a platter. Garnish with pickled ginger and serve with soy sauce.

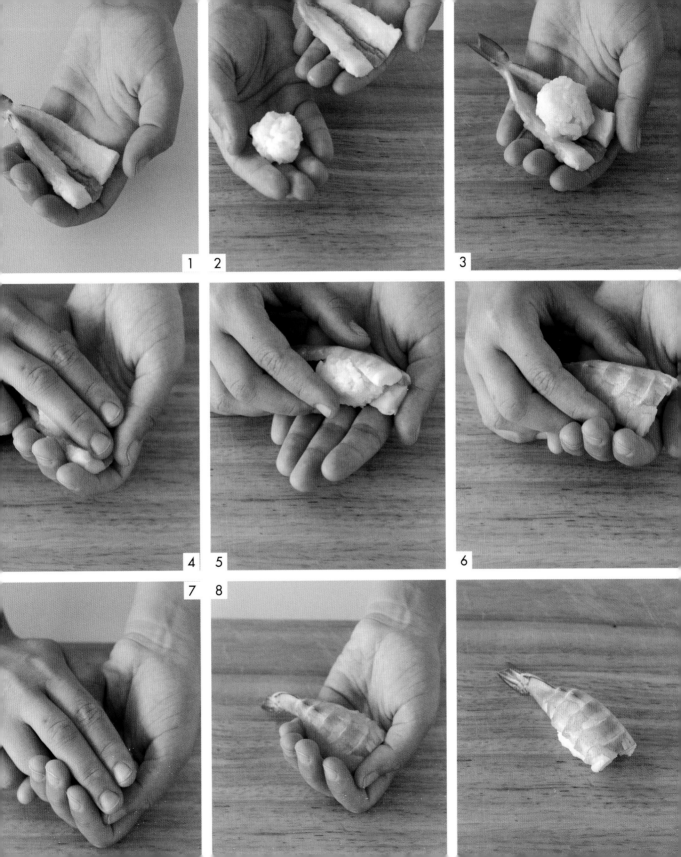

1 2 3

4 5 6

7 8

Tomato and Avocado Nigiri-zushi

Ingredients

½ tomato
*½ avocado, de-seeded and
    sliced*
*3½oz (100g) sushi rice, divided
    into 5 portions*
*5 nori strips, about ¾in (2cm)
    wide and 4in (10cm) long*
*mayonnaise or sesame seeds,
    for decoration*

Utensils

*chopping board, knife, tezu (or
    water in a bowl)*

makes 5 pieces

1. Slice tomato and avocado to make 5 pieces.
2. Dampen your fingers with tezu, pick up 1 sushi rice portion in your
   hand and gently shape into an oval/rectangular form. Place on a dry
   plate. Repeat with remaining rice.
3. Arrange tomato slices on the sushi shape and top with avocado.
4. Wrap nori band over sushi, encasing tomato and avocado.
5. Decorate with mayonnaise or sesame seeds if you like.

Cucumber Nigiri-zushi

makes 5 pieces

1. Place cucumber on a board and with a peeler, peel 1 strip of outer skin along length of cucumber and discard. Using the peeler cut 5 thin strips.
2. Moisten your fingers with tezu, pick up sushi rice in your hand and gently shape into an oval/rectangular form. Place on a dry plate. Repeat with remaining rice.
3. Starting underneath the sushi rice, wrap the cucumber strip over the top, along the length of the rice, leaving the end hanging free, creating a sweeping effect
4. Wrap a nori strip across the top of the sushi and cucumber, making a band. Seal ends together underneath.
5. Top with ume-boshi paste on nori as decoration.

Ingredients
1 Lebanese cucumber
3½oz (100g) sushi rice, divided
  into 5 portions
5 nori strips, ¾in (2cm) wide x
  4in (10cm) long
3 teaspoons ume-boshi
  (Japanese salted plum) paste
  (sold in a tube at Japanese
  grocery shops)

Utensils
chopping board, vegetable
  peeler (swivel-action peelers
  are preferable)

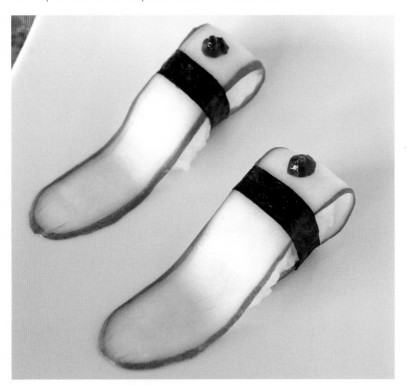

Gunkan with Teriyaki Chicken and Alfalfa

Ingredients

1 sheet of nori
2½oz (80g) sushi rice, divided into 4 portions
a handful of alfalfa or small salad leaves
1¾oz (50g) cooked marinated chicken teriyaki, chopped finely (see Teriyaki Chicken recipe)

Utensils

scissors, tezu (bowl of water)

makes 4 pieces

1. Cut nori about 1in (2.5cm) wide and 6in (15cm) long with scissors.
2. Moisten your fingers with tezu, pick up one portion of sushi rice in your hand and gently shape into an oval/rectangular form. Place on a dry plate. Repeat with remaining rice (see photo 1).
3. With rough side of nori facing rice, wrap a strip of nori all round rice and gently press overlapping edges to secure. If they do not stick together, put a couple of grains of crushed rice in between the layers to hold ends together (see photos 2 and 3).
4. With a spoon or fingers, arrange alfalfa leaves and chicken on top of rice inside the ring of nori (see photos 4, 5 and 6).

123
Nigiri-zushi

Corn Mayonnaise Gunkan

Ingredients

1 sheet of nori
1½oz (40g) corn kernel, frozen or fresh, cooked and cooled
2 teaspoons mayonnaise
2½oz (80g) sushi rice, divided into 4 portions
1 teaspoon parsley or chives, chopped

Utensils

scissors, bowl, plate, spoon, tezu (bowl of water)

makes 4 pieces

1. Cut nori about 1in (2.5cm) wide and 6in (15cm) long with scissors.
2. Mix corn and mayonnaise in a bowl.
3. Moisten your fingers with tezu, pick up sushi rice in your hand and gently shape into an oval/rectangular form. Place on a dry plate. Repeat with remaining rice.
4. With rough side of nori facing rice, wrap nori all round rice and gently press overlapping edges to secure.
5. With a spoon or fingers, arrange corn on top of rice inside the ring of nori.
6. Sprinkle parsley or chives over the top.

Modern Gunkan Wrapped with Cucumber

Ingredients

1 Lebanese cucumber
2½oz (80g) sushi rice, divided into 4 portions
2 small cherry tomatoes, sliced
2 black or green olives, sliced
other toppings: anchovies, cheese, or any other topping of your own choice.

Utensils

vegetable peeler, small knife, tezu (bowl of water)

makes 4 pieces

1. Using a vegetable peeler, peel off a wide, lengthways slice of cucumber skin and discard. Place cucumber on a chopping board, cut side up, hold firmly, and with the peeler, cut a paper-thin slice about 1in (3cm) wide and 4in (10cm) long. (This strip will have a narrow green outer edge of skin and white flesh in the centre. The skin helps the cucumber to stick to the rice.) Cut halfway into one end of the cucumber slice (see photo 1).
2. Repeat to make three more slices.
3. Turn the cucumber slice on its side and slide the other end into the cut half (see photo 2). Repeat with remaining slices.
4. Moisten your fingers with tezu, pick up sushi rice in your hand and gently shape into an oval/rectangular form. Place on a dry plate. Repeat with remaining rice.
5. Place the rice balls into the middle of the cucumber (see photo 5).
6. Top with tomato and olive (see photo 6).

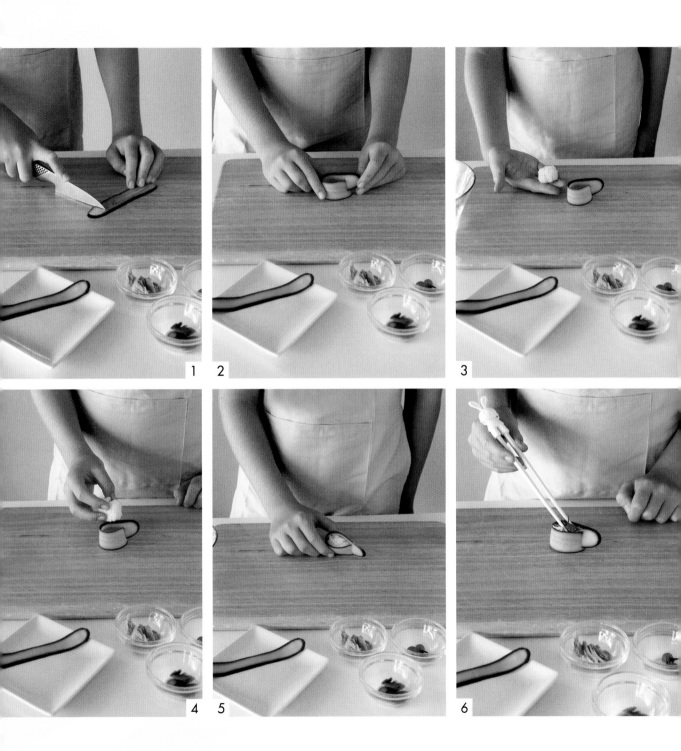

1 2 3

4 5 6

127
Nigiri-zushi

Modern Gunkan Wrapped with Carrot

Ingredients

1 large carrot
2½oz (80g) sushi rice, divided into 4 portions
2 teaspoons canned tuna (squeeze out the liquid from the tuna)
1 pinch small salad leaves
Soy Sauce Jelly (see recipe)

Utensils

vegetable peeler, tezu (bowl of water), plate,

makes 4 pieces

1. Using a vegetable peeler, peel the skin from the carrot and discard. Place carrot on a chopping board, cut side up, hold firmly, and with the peeler, cut a wide, lengthways of carrot.
2. Repeat to make 3 more slices.
3. Moisten your fingers with tezu, pick up sushi rice in your hand and gently shape into an oval/rectangular form. Place on a dry plate. Repeat with remaining rice.
4. Wrap a carrot strip around outside of each rice shape, either tucking the outer end over the inner end against the rice, or using a toothpick to secure the ends.
5. Top with tuna, salad leaves and soy sauce jelly.

Temari-zushi (Hand-ball Sushi)

Ingredients

3½oz (100g) sushi rice
toppings of your choice:
    2 jumbo shrimp (king
    prawns), cooked, peeled,
    deveined and butterflied (see
    Fish and Seafood section)
    1 small slice prosciutto or
    any other ham
    1 small piece of smoked
    salmon
    1 cheese slice
2 nori strips, for decoration
parmesan cheese, for garnish
dill, for garnish
1 stalk parsley, for garnish
soy sauce, for serving

Utensils

bowl, rice paddle or spoon,
    5 sheets of plastic wrap
    (6in/15cm long)

Temari-zushi is slightly different from nigiri-zushi because you use plastic wrap to shape the sushi into balls.

makes 5 balls

1. Roughly divide sushi rice into 5.
2. Lay a sheet of plastic wrap on a board.
3. Place a topping ingredient, such as jumbo shrimp, onto the plastic wrap (see photo 1).
4. Take a ball of sushi rice and place it in the middle of the topping (see photo 2).
5. Draw edges of plastic wrap over the topping and rice and twist it together and shape into a ball (see photos 3 and 4).
6. Repeat with other ingredients.
7. Just before serving, remove plastic wrap and decorate with nori strip, parmesan cheese, dill or parsley (see photos 5 and 6).
8. Serve with soy sauce.

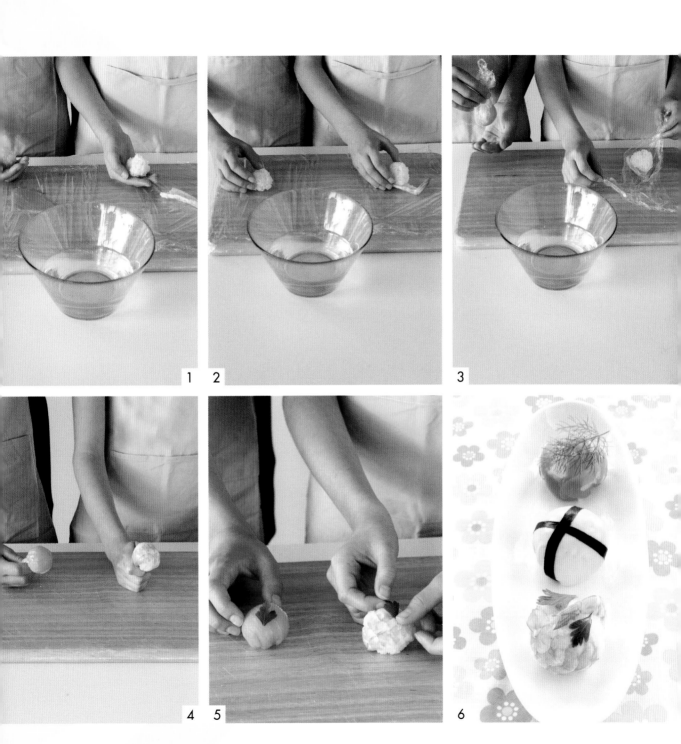

Nigiri-zushi

Caterpillar Roll

Ingredients

5oz (140g) sushi rice

1 teaspoon yukari (seasoned dried shiso) or other rice sprinkles

12 mint leaves for feet

7 cherry tomato halves

2 (small circle) pieces of nori for decoration as eyes

2 chives for antennas

7 drops of mayonnaise

soy sauce for serving

Utensils

bowl, rice paddle or spoon, 7 sheets of plastic wrap (6in/15cm long), plate

makes 7 balls

1. Place sushi rice in a bowl and sprinkle on yukari. Combine well.
2. Roughly divide sushi rice into 7.
3. Lay a sheet of plastic wrap on a board.
4. Draw edges of plastic wrap over rice, while twisting together and shape into a ball.
5. Lay the mint leaves down in pairs, in one line on the plate. Remove plastic wrap and line up all balls to form a caterpillar.
6. Place tomato halves on top of the rice balls then place a drop of mayonnaise on the top of the tomato.
7. At one end, arrange nori to make eyes and chives for antennas, to make a head
8. Serve with soy sauce.

Inari-zushi

Inari-zushi is a pocket of deep-fried tofu skin called abura-age, stuffed with sushi rice. Inari is the name of the Fox God of rice, agriculture and fertility. It is believed that the Fox God likes to eat abura-age, which is the colour of fox's fur.

The abura-age is deep-fried, thin tofu which can be bought from the freezer section in Japanese or Asian grocery shops. To prepare it for inari-zushi, it needs to be further cooked in a mixture of dashi, sugar, mirin and soy sauce. Sometimes you can buy it already cooked, or it can be cooked at home. This cooking gives it a unique sweet and savoury flavour. Although it is only a thin sheet, after it is cooked, it is possible to gently separate it into 2 layers using your thumbs, to create small pouches. It is either square or oblong, and can be sliced in a number of ways. The abura-age pouches are stuffed with sushi rice and may be sealed up or left open, with some toppings.

Preparation of Abura-age for Inari-zushi

Ingredients
3 abura-age tofu (not cooked), 2 x 4in (5 x 10cm)
1½ cups dashi stock
3 tablespoons superfine (caster) sugar
2 tablespoons mirin
2 tablespoons soy sauce

Utensils
knife or scissors, saucepan, chopping board, cooking chopsticks or rolling pin, tongs (or mesh ladle), sheet of baking paper cut to fit inside saucepan, spatula

1. With a knife or scissors, cut each piece of rectangular abura-age tofu in half to make 2 squares (see photos 1, 2 and 3).
2. To remove the excess oil from the abura-age tofu, bring 2 cups of water to boil in a saucepan. Boil the abura-age in the water for a few minutes. Drain the tofu, place on a chopping board and roll with the cooking chopstick or a rolling pin, to squeeze out the water and unwanted oil. Be careful—it might squirt you! (see photos 4 and 5).
3. Using your thumbs, carefully open the abura-age along the cuts to make 6 pockets.
4. Put dashi into a saucepan and bring it to the boil.
5. Using tongs or a mesh ladle, put in abura-age tofu. Add sugar, mirin and soy sauce (see photos 6 and 7).
6. To keep abura-age submerged while cooking, place the cut sheet of baking paper on top. Bring the mixture to the boil and simmer over low heat for about 10 minutes. Remove from heat and allow to stand until liquid is cool (see photos 8 and 9).
7. Using a spatula, remove abura-age tofu from pan and squeeze to remove excess liquid.

Basic Inari-zushi

Ingredients

12oz (360g) sushi rice
*3 prepared abura-age tofu cut
in half to make 6 pouches
(see Preparation of abura-
age for inari-zushi)*

Utensils

*tezu (bowl of water or vinagar
water)*

makes 6 pieces

1. Divide sushi rice into 6 portions.
2. With moist hands, lightly form rice portions into small balls, do not squeeze hard.
3. Fill tofu loosely with sushi rice. If you fill the pouch too tightly, it may break.
4. Tuck top ends of pouch inside, leaving rice exposed, or overlap to cover rice.

You may use sushi rice mixed with 1 teaspoon roasted white sesame seeds if you like.

Log-shaped Inari-zushi

Ingredients

12oz (360g) sushi rice

3 prepared abura-age tofu pouches (see Preparation of abura-age for inari-zushi), sliced horizontally

20 cooked edamame, without pods (green soy beans, available in frozen section at Japanese groceries)

1 teaspoon yukari (Japanese red basil sprinkles)

Utensils

2 small bowls, 2 spoons, 6 sheets of plastic wrap, chopping board and a small knife, tezu (bowl of water or vinegar water)

makes 6 pieces

1. Divide sushi rice into two bowls.
2. In one bowl add edamame and combine with a moistened spoon.
3. In the other bowl add yukari sprinkles and mix with a moistened spoon.
4. Roughly divide each bowl of sushi rice into 3 portions.
5. With wet fingers, make each portion into a log shape and place it into the tofu pouch.
6. Tuck top ends of pouch inside.
7. Place plastic wrap on a dry board and put inari-zushi in the centre.
8. Wrap and shape like a log.
9. Repeat with other pouches.
10. Leave for 20 minutes to set.
11. Before serving, with a small knife cut into half slightly diagonally,

Hana-inari

Ingredients

1 small Lebanese cucumber

1 small carrot

*8 prepared abura-age tofu
pouches (see Preparation of
abura-age for inari-zushi)*

10½oz (300g) sushi rice

1½oz (40g) gari (pickled ginger)

*1 teaspoon egg mimosa (see
Garnishes and Decorations)*

24 green peas, cooked

24 capers

*8 snow pea sprouts or green
salad leaves*

Utensils

*tablespoon or soup spoon,
chopping board, knife, peeler,
tezu (bowl of water)*

makes 8 pieces

1. Place cucumber on a chopping board and with a vegetable peeler slice lengthways. Prepare 8 long slices.
2. With a peeler, peel carrot and as with cucumber, slice and prepare 8 long slices.
3. Gently open a tofu pouch.
4. Dip a tablespoon in water and spoon sushi rice into an inari pouch.
5. Make small rolls with cucumber and carrot.
6. Arrange on the top of sushi rice along with gari.
7. Arrange egg mimosa, green peas and capers on top.
8. Insert snow pea sprout beside them.

Chirashi-zushi

Chirashi-zushi is sushi rice and toppings, served in a bowl. It is a dish for celebrating the change of season and for happy occasions. Typically sushi rice is mixed with various ingredients, and then topped with seasonal vegetables, fish or egg. You can make chirashi-zushi with left-over ingredients. This is good for school lunches, but do not use raw fish.

Chirashi-zushi in cups

For a party, serve chirashi-zushi in a small cup with a spoon and add your choice of ingredients.

Chirashi-zushi

Serves 4

1. To prepare shiitake mushrooms, soak dried shiitake mushrooms in two cups of water in a saucepan until soft, for about 30 minutes. Once softened, remove from saucepan and with a small knife trim off the stems.
2. Replace mushrooms in the water. Add soy sauce and caster or raw sugar to the saucepan.
3. Bring it to the boil, turn the heat low and cook for 20 minutes.
4. Remove from the heat and leave until cooled down.
5. With your hands, lightly squeeze shiitake mushrooms and place on a chopping board.
6. Using a small knife, slice shiitake mushrooms.
7. Cook carrots in boiling water for 3 minutes and drain.
8. To prepare jumbo shrimp, remove the head and shell without cutting off the tail. Remove vein with a bamboo skewer.
9. Crack eggs into a bowl and beat with sugar and salt until dissolved.
10. In a Teflon-coated frying pan, cook the egg over a low heat, scrambling with chopsticks or a wooden spatula until tiny lumps form. Set aside. (When you use a non-stick pan use a few drops of oil before cooking.)
11. If using frozen kamaboko, cook first in boiling water.
12. Place sushi rice in a bowl, mix in the denbu and scatter the mushrooms, carrots, shrimp, scrambled egg, kamaboko fish cake on top. Serve with soy sauce.
13. Other ingredients which can be added: cooked English spinach, lotus root, okra, broccoli, grilled eel (unagi), beni-shoga (pickled red ginger), avocado, smoked salmon, etc.

Ingredients

2–4 dried shiitake mushrooms
2 cups water
1 tablespoon soy sauce
1 tablespoon superfine (caster) sugar or raw sugar
2 tablespoons fresh or frozen green peas or snow peas, precooked
4 flower-shaped carrot (see Garnishes and Decorations)
4 cooked jumbo shrimp (king prawns)
1 egg
½ teaspoon superfine (caster) or raw sugar
pinch of salt
drop of vegetable oil
14oz (400g) sushi rice
1 tablespoon denbu (lightly mashed fish)
4 slices kamaboko fish cake
soy sauce for serving

Utensils

small knife, kitchen knife, chopping board, 2 saucepans, a vegetable cookie cutter, small non-stick (Teflon-coated) frying pan, disposable chopsticks or wooden spatula, large serving bowl

Seafood Chirashi-zushi

Ingredients

21oz (600g) sushi rice
*1¾oz (50g) lotus roots plus 1
    teaspoon rice vinegar and
    2 cups water for soaking*
2 tablespoons rice vinegar
*1 teaspoon superfine (caster)
    sugar*
pinch of salt
*3½oz (100g) tuna or salmon
    (sashimi quality)*
1½oz (40g) salmon caviar
*1 Japanese thick omelette (see
    Preparing Fillings for Nori
    Rolls)*
a few bean sprouts

Utensils

*peeler, knife, chopping board,
    saucepan, small serving
    bowls*

Serves 4

1. With a peeler, peel lotus root and with a slicer or a knife slice lotus root thinly. Soak in vinegar and water for 5 minutes.
2. Prepare vinegar mixture by combining rice vinegar, sugar and a pinch of salt in a plastic container.
3. Bring a saucepan of water to the boil.
4. Take lotus root out of vinegar water, place it in the boiling water, cook for 2 minutes then drain. Transfer lotus root into the vinegar mixture and leave for 30 minutes. Strain before adding to rice.
5. You can colour lotus pink by adding food colouring or natural colouring, such as beetroot juice to the vinegar mixture.
6. With a knife slice tuna into 2/3in (1.5cm) thick slices.
7. Slice omelette into 2/3in (1.5cm) strips.
8. Place rice in individual small bowls.
9. Arrange tuna, salmon caviar, lotus roots, omelette and bean sprouts on top.
10. Serve with soy sauce

Salmon can be used instead of tuna. Other possible ingredients include jumbo shrimp (king prawns) or cucumber.

New-style Chirashi-zushi

Ingredients

14oz (600g) sushi rice
4 cherry tomatoes
4 strips of red capsicum, diced
½ pink grapefruit or a handful
   of blueberries
4 chicory or salad leaves
4 walnuts
2 anchovies (or salami if you
   prefer)
parmesan cheese, shaved
1 teaspoon Soy Sauce Jelly (see
   recipe)

Utensils

small knife, chopping board,
   wooden spoon, non-stick
   frying pan

Serves 4

1. With a small knife, cut cherry tomatoes in half.
2. Peel grapefruit and separate segments. Discard skin and cut each
    segment into 3 pieces.
3. Tear chicory into bite-sized pieces.
4. Chop anchovies or salami.
5. Add sushi rice and all of the ingredients in a serving bowl and toss
    with a wooden spoon. Divide the rice between the 4 salad leaves.
6. Shave parmesan cheese over the sushi and decorate with soy sauce
    jelly.

Temaki-zushi

Temaki-zushi, hand-wrapped sushi cones, is hand-rolled sheet of nori filled with sushi rice and a variety of other ingredients. It is the easiest type of sushi to make at home. You can also use other wrap ingredients, such as omelettes, rice paper or salad leaves.

Temaki-zushi is suitable for a special lunch/dinner or a casual party for people who enjoy making sushi to their own taste. The method is simple; you just need to prepare sushi rice and fillings, then set the table. Prepare the fillings ahead of time and lay them out attractively in separate bowls or on one large platter, on the table. Also it doesn't take much time to adjust the amount of the ingredients.

If you're hosting a temaki-zushi party, give your guests a little guidance on how to make the cone and then let them try it for themselves.

Sample Guidance Note:

After washing your hands, pick a sheet of nori and spoon sushi rice on the centre, slightly flatten and spread. Choose fillings and arrange on the rice along with your choice of sauce or paste. Then wrap up.

Temaki-zushi

Ingredients

4–6 whole nori sheets, halved or quartered

sauces and dressings, such as soy sauce or mayonnaise, (see Dressings in Basic Techniques)

3–4 cups sushi rice, in a large bowl with a scoop

more than 3 fillings chosen depending on your preference

Utensils

Basically there are no utensils needed for making temaki, only for preparing your fillings. When preparing the fillings you will need: small (wooden) spoon for serving rice, dampened hand-towels are useful to clean your hands. Set them beside individual plates.

serves 1 (makes 4 slices)

For temaki-zushi, a half or quarter-sized nori sheet is used.

1. To make half-sized nori, fold a whole nori sheet into half and cut along the folded line with your hands or scissors.
2. To make quarter-sized nori sheet, fold a whole nori into half lengthways. Join one end and the top of the other side together lengthways and fold into half slantwise to make a fold. Cut into half along the fold line.
3. Or just fold into half and quarter to make lines and cut along them to make square sheets.

How to prepare ingredients:

Choose a variety of fillings—whatever you want (see Preparing fillings for nori rolls).

- Vegetables: carrot, watercress, cucumber, green salad, avocado,
- Meat: Chicken, jumbo shrimp (king prawn), crab meat stick, omelette, grilled eel, ham, salmon (smoked, tinned or fresh), tuna (fresh or tinned)

How to roll temaki with a half-sized nori sheet:

1. In your left hand hold a sheet of nori horizontally and with a wet spoon put sushi rice in the centre and slightly spread it over the nori sheet in a line across one corner (see photos 1, 2 and 3).
2. Add a little mayonnaise to taste. Place any combination of the fillings on top (see photo 4).
3. With your right hand wrap up the nori, making a cone shape (see photo 5 and 6).
4. Spoon caviar on top if you like.
5. Serve with soy sauce.

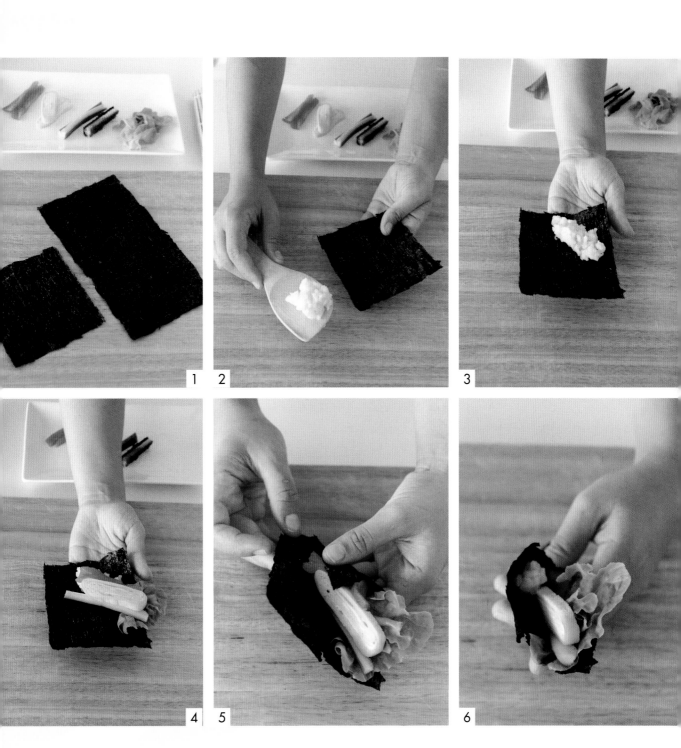

1 2 3 4 5 6

153
Temaki-zushi

Temaki-zushi in Crêpe

Ingredients

1 cup all-purpose (plain) flour
1 cup water
1 egg
vegetable oil for cooking
2 tablespoons sushi rice
6 crêpes, halved
1 crab stick, halved
2 avocado slices
2 small salad leaves
1 tablespoon mayonnaise

Utensils

bowl, chopsticks or fork,
*   strainer, spatula, non-stick*
*   (Teflon) frying pan, ladle*

makes 12

1. In a bowl, add flour, water and egg.
2.   Mix with chopsticks or a fork.
3. Strain with a strainer into a bowl.
4. Rest for 30 minutes.
5. Heat a non-stick frying pan over low heat. If you don't have a non-stick pan, add some vegetable oil.
6. When the pan is hot, ladle one-sixth of the batter mixture into the pan, moving the pan around so that the batter covers the base of the pan. When the surface begins to set, gently insert the spatula under the edge and turn over to cook other side. Remove and set aside to cool.
7. Repeat to make a total of 6 crêpes.
8. Cut crêpes in half.
9. Spread mayonnaise on the centre of each crêpe.
10. Arrange salad leaf, rice and half a crab stick and avocado on each crêpe.
11. Roll them up, making cone shapes.

Fukusa-zushi (Wrapped Sushi in Omelette)

Ingredients

5½oz (160g) sushi rice

1 tablespoon canned tuna or
  1 teaspoon chopped
  anchovies

½ teaspoon soy sauce

½ teaspoon white roasted
  sesame seeds

option: you may mix rice with
  grated ginger, chopped fresh
  ginger, green peas, etc.

4 blanched chives or mitsuba

4 thin omelettes (see Preparing
  Fillings for Nori Rolls)

Utensils

bowl, fork or whisk, spoon,
  non-stick frying pan (about
  17 cm wide), ladle, spatula

makes 4

1. Using a moistened spoon, mix sushi rice with tuna, soy sauce and
    sesame seeds in a bowl.
2. Lay omelette on a dry plate and spoon rice on the centre. Wrap rice
    in omelette, folding corners like a parcel. Tie a chive around the
    centre.

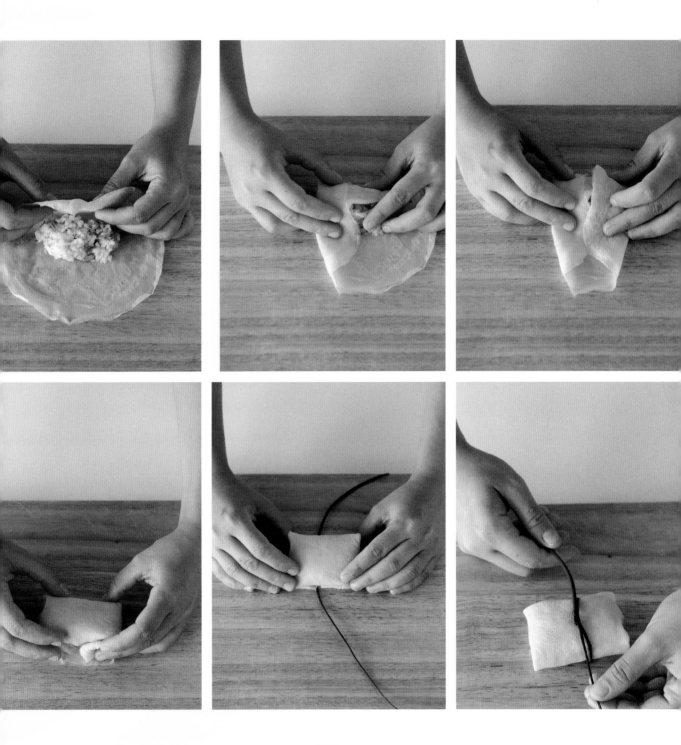

Fukusa-zushi

Oshi-zushi or Hako-zushi

Oshi-zushi (pressed sushi) or hako-zushi (box sushi) is sushi rice that has been pressed into a box mould, with other ingredients as a topping. The mould is removed and layers are cut into bite-sized pieces. The sushi mould consists of a box with two lids. But it is only available from a specialised Japanese shop.

Here we use a small cake tin about 5½ x 2¾in (14 x 7cm).

Makes 1 box

1. Arrange plastic wrap around the base and sides of the tin.
2. Arrange smoked salmon slices on the bottom.
3. Put the sushi rice up to the top of the tin.
4. If you have another tin of the same size, use the bottom of the empty tin to press firmly on the top of the full tin; or use a spoon to set evenly.
5. Carefully turn it over onto a dry chopping board.
6. With moisten knife, slice into 6 pieces.
7. With moisten hand arrange on a plate.
8. Decorate with ricotta cheese and mustered cress on top.
9. You may use grilled eel instead of smoked salmon.

Ingredients

1–1¾oz (30–50g) smoked
   salmon*
3–3½oz (90–100g) sushi rice
1 tablespoon ricotta cheese
mustard cress or green salad
   leaves for decoration

Utensils

plastic wrap, 1–2 cake tins or
   box mould (5½ x 2¾in/14 x
   7cm), chopping board, knife

Moulded/Cup Sushi

Ingredients

1¾oz (50g) broccoli
½ teaspoon olive oil
5–6oz (140–180g) sushi rice or
*   pink rice*
soy sauce for serving

Utensils

2 small cups (size around
*   2–2¼in/5–6cm diameter*
*   and 2in/5cm high. Smaller*
*   cups are easier to handle.),*
*   saucepan, strainer, chopping*
*   board, knife, bowl, spatula,*
*   serving plate*

This is an easy and colourful sushi. Just mix sushi rice with other ingredients and mould with a small cup or cookie cutter.

Broccoli Cup Sushi

makes 2 cups

1. Divide broccoli into small pieces. Cook in boiling water for 1 minute and strain. Refresh under running water and drain well. Keep two pieces for decoration and chop others with a knife on a chopping board.
2. Place chopped broccoli in a small bowl and mix with olive oil.
3. With a moistened rice spatula combine sushi rice with chopped broccoli.
4. Slightly wet one cup and using a rice spatula, stuff with sushi rice. With the other empty cup, press to firm the rice.
5. Turn sushi upside down on a serving plate and remove from the cup by tapping the bottom with your hand.
6. Top with a piece of broccoli as a decoration.

Tobiko-cup Sushi

Ingredients
5oz (140g) sushi rice
2 teaspoons tobiko (flying fish roe)
2 teaspoons cottage cheese
soy sauce for serving

Utensils
bowl, spatula, 2 small cups (size around 2–2¼in/5–6cm diameter and 2in/5cm high. Smaller cups are easier to handle.),

makes 2 cups

1. Place sushi rice and tobiko in a bowl and combine with a moistened rice spatula.
2. Slightly wet cup and stuff with sushi rice using a rice spatula. With another empty cup press to firm.
3. Turn sushi upside down on a serving plate and remove from the cup by tapping the bottom with your hand.
4. Top with cottage cheese.

Tuna and Cucumber Cup Sushi
makes 2 cups

Ingredients
5oz (140g) sushi rice
2/3oz (20g) canned tuna
¾oz (25g) Lebanese cucumber, chopped
2 teaspoons mayonnaise
soy sauce for serving

Utensils
2 small cups (size around 2–2¼in/5–6cm diameter and 2in/5cm high. Smaller cups are easier to handle.)

1. Place sushi rice, tuna and cucumber in a bowl and combine with a moistened rice spatula.
2. Slightly wet one cup and stuff with sushi rice using a rice spatula. With the other empty cup press to firm.
3. Turn sushi upside down on a serving plate and remove from the cup by tapping the bottom with your hand.
4. Top with mayonnaise.

Corn Cup Sushi
Makes 2 cups

Ingredients
1¾oz (50g) corn kernels
¼ teaspoon butter
5oz (140g) sushi rice
1 tablespoon shredded nori, for
    garnish
soy sauce for serving

Utensils
saucepan, knife, spatula,
    serving plate, 2 small cups
    (size around 2–2¼in/5–6cm
    diameter and 2in/5cm high.
    Smaller cups are easier to
    handle.)

1. Cook corn in boiling water. Remove from pan, cut off kernels with a knife (adult supervision required) and mix with butter while still warm.
2. Place sushi rice and corn in a bowl and combine with a moistened rice spatula.
3. Slightly wet cup and stuff with sushi rice, using a rice spatula. With another empty cup press to firm.
4. Turn sushi upside down on a serving plate and remove from the cup by tapping the bottom with your hand.
5. Top with nori strips.

Heart-shaped Sushi with Smoked Salmon

makes 1 heart-shaped sushi

Ingredients

½ cup sushi rice (the amount you use will depend on the size of the cutter)

pinch of yukari or your favourite sprinkles

small slice of smoked salmon

¼ slice lime/lemon

Utensils

bowl, rice spatula or tablespoon, small heart-shaped cookie cutter or mould, serving plate, spoon, tezu (a bowl of water)

1. Place sushi rice and yukari in a bowl and combine with a moistened rice spatula.
2. Immerse a small heart-shaped cookie cutter in a bowl of water.
3. Slightly drain water out of cutter and transfer it onto the centre of a plate.
4. Stuff with sushi rice with a moistened spatula/spoon.
5. Holding cutter with one hand and pushing the top of the rice with your other hand, carefully remove cutter from the formed rice.
6. Arrange smoked salmon on top and add the slice of lemon.

Tulip-shaped Sushi with Pink Denbu Flakes

makes 1 small tulip-shaped sushi

Ingredients

1/4–½ cup sushi rice (the amount you need depends on the size of the cutter)

1 teaspoon denbu (fish and sugar, see Japanese groceries)

1 mint leaves, with a stalk

Utensils

tezu (a bowl of water), rice spatula or tablespoon, small tulip-shaped cookie cutter or mould, serving plate, spoon

1. Immerse a cutter in a bowl of water and slightly drain water out of cutter.
2. Transfer it onto the plate.
3. Stuff the mould with sushi rice using a moistened spatula or spoon.
4. Spread denbu over the top.
5. Carefully remove the cutter from the formed rice.
6. Arrange mint leaves as the stem of the flower.
7. Alternatively you can choose pink sushi rice/coloured sushi rice instead of denbu.

Other Sushi

This is a sandwich with a difference. Instead of bread, use sushi rice with a sheet of nori. Fillings can be as varied and versatile as you like.

Ham and Cheese Sushi Sandwich

makes 1 sandwich

Ingredients

2 sheets of quarter-size nori
4oz (120g) sushi rice
1 slice ham
1 slice cheese
couple of small salad leaves
mayonnaise, optional (spread it
* on the rice if you like)*
gari (pickled ginger), to serve
soy sauce, to serve

Utensils

chopping board, tezu (bowl of
* water or vinaigrette water),*
* spoon, bamboo sushi mat, a*
* knife*

1. Place nori sheets on a dry surface or chopping board.
2. Spoon sushi rice over each nori and with moist fingers spread evenly.
3. Arrange ham, cheese, salad leaves on one of sushi rice with nori.
4. Top with the other sheet of sushi rice with nori.
5. Place sushi mat on the nori and give a gentle press with your hand.
6. With a knife, slice diagonally to make triangle sushi sandwiches.
7. Serve with gari (pickled ginger) and soy sauce.

Egg and Cucumber Sushi Sandwich

Ingredients

2 sheets of quarter-size nori
4oz (120g) sushi rice
1 boiled egg, mashed
1 teaspoon mayonnaise
3 slices cucumber
3 slices tomato
soy sauce, to serve
Other possible fillings: Crab
  sticks, shredded carrot.

Utensils

chopping board, spoon, tezu
  (bowl of water), knife

Makes 1 sandwich

1. Place nori sheet on a dry surface or chopping board.
2. Spoon sushi rice over each nori and with moist fingers spread evenly.
3. Mix the egg with the mayonnaise. Spread the mayonnaise on the rice.
4. Arrange the cucumber and tomato slices on one of sushi rice with nori.
5. Top with the other sheet of sushi rice with nori.
6. Place sushi mat on the nori and give a gentle press with your hand.
7. With a knife, slice diagonally to make triangle sushi sandwiches.
8. Serve with soy sauce.

Instead of the boiled egg, you can use canned tuna, salmon, etc.

Soup

Dashi (Stock)

Ingredients

17½fl oz (500ml) water
2 sheets of 2in (5cm) square dried kelp, wiped with a dry cloth
2 teaspoons dried bonito flakes

Utensils

saucepan, fine strainer

makes 17½fl oz (500ml) dashi

1. Soak kelp in water for at least 15 minutes in a saucepan, then slowly bring to the boil. Remove from the heat and set aside for 10 minutes. Discard the kelp.
2. Return to the heat and bring to the boil.
3. Add bonito flakes, turn the heat to low and simmer for 1 minute.
4. Remove from the heat and when the bonito flakes have sunk, sieve the stock with a fine strainer.

Miso Soup

Ingredients

4 cups dashi or water (see Japanese Groceries section)
¼ small packet silken tofu, cubed
1 pinch of dried wakame-seaweed, soaked in water
2 tablespoons light brown miso paste
2 tablespoons water
1 scallion (spring onion) stem, chopped

Utensils

saucepan, small cup, ladle

Serve 4

1. Bring dashi to boil in a saucepan
2. Add tofu and wakame.
3. Mix miso and water in a small cup. Add to the saucepan.
4. Simmer for a couple of minutes.
5. With a ladle, pour the soup into individual bowls.
6. Sprinkle spring onion over the top.
7. You could also add in chopped carrot, zucchini, shiitake mushroom, shimeji-mushroom, enoki-mushroom.

Snacks and Desserts

Edamame

Edamame (fresh green soy beans) are quite popular with sushi.

Fresh edamame are rarely found outside Japan but you can find frozen edamame in Japanese or Asian grocery shops.

There are salted and unsalted edamame, so you can choose whichever you prefer. To prepare, simply boil in some water or use microwave oven.

Gari (Pickled Ginger) (see Japanese Groceries)

Popcorn in Sweet Soy Sauce

makes 1 bowl of popcorn

Ingredients
1 teaspoon vegetable oil
1 tablespoon popcorn kernels
1 tablespoon butter
1 tablespoon honey or corn syrup
1 tablespoon soy sauce
1 tablespoon raw sugar

Utensils
covered saucepan, bowl, wooden spoon

1. Drop oil in a saucepan and heat up on medium heat.
2. Put popcorn kernels into the oil and cover the pan with a lid.
3. When the kernels start to pop, remove from heat and count 30 seconds.
4. Return the pan to the heat.
5. Once the popping starts again, gently shake the pan, moving it back and forth for about 30 seconds.
6. Slightly raise the lid at an angle to let the steam out of the pan for 30 seconds.
7. Remove from the heat and transfer into a bowl.
8. To make sweet soy sauce, combine butter, honey, soy sauce and sugar in a saucepan.
9. Bring mixture to the boil over low heat and cook for 3 minutes, stirring continuously with a wooden spoon.
10. Drizzle over the popcorn.
11. Be careful! The sauce is very hot and can burn you.

Meringue Sushi

Ingredients

2 egg whites
½ cup superfine (caster) sugar
1 teaspoon cornflour, sifted
½ teaspoon white vinegar or lemon juice
selection of seasonal fruits, sliced
1 teaspoon melted chocolate in a small jug

Utensils

clean bowl, hand mixer or electric mixer, wooden spoon, sheet of baking paper, baking tray, tablespoon, spatula or table knife

makes about 12 pieces

1. Preheat the oven to 250°F (120°C).
2. Place the egg whites in a clean bowl or an electric mixer bowl.
3. Beat until soft peaks form.
4. Gradually add the sugar and beat until stiff peaks form.
5. Add cornflour and vinegar, and fold through using a wooden spoon.
6. Lay baking paper on a baking tray.
7. Scoop up a tablespoon of meringue, and with another tablespoon held in your other hand, shape up the meringue and gently slide it onto the baking sheet. Try to keep the dollop of meringue in even rows.
8. Using a sliding motion, gently flatten the top of each meringue with a table knife.
9. Place in the oven and bake for 25-30 minutes.
10. Turn the oven off and allow the meringues to cool while still in the oven.
11. Arrange meringues on individual plates or a large plate topped with sliced seasonal fruit.
12. Serve with melted chocolate.

Cream Cheese Roll Cake

Ingredients

5oz (150g) tinned citrus fruit,
 well drained to remove liquid,
 or any seasonal fruits

3 eggs

2oz (65g) superfine (caster)
 sugar

2 tablespoons milk

1¾oz (50g) all-purpose (plain)
 flour, sifted

2oz (60g) cream cheese, at
 room temperature

1½ tablespoons superfine
 (caster) sugar

3½fl oz (100ml) thickened
 cream, at room temperature

Utensils

kitchen paper, sheet of baking
 paper, 11½ x 11½in (29 x
 29cm) baking dish, saucepan,
 3 bowls, spatula, hand mixer
 or whisk

1. Lay citrus fruits on kitchen paper on a tray so they are well drained.
2. Preheat the oven to 375°F (190°C).
3. Place baking paper on the baking dish.
4. Half-fill saucepan with hot water.
5. Break eggs into a bowl, add sugar and place it over the hot water to double boil. Whisk with a hand mixer over gentle heat until the colour becomes creamy.
6. Remove the mixture from the double boiler and add milk and flour.
7. Whisk until combined well.
8. Spread the mixture onto the baking paper on the baking dish and make the surface even with a spatula.
9. Bake it for 12 minutes.
10. Once baked, transfer onto a cooling rack and allow it to cool down.
11. In the meantime, place cream cheese and sugar in a bowl and whisk until creamy.
12. Whip the cream in another bowl. Add half of the cream cheese into the whipped cream and mix, then add the rest and combine well. Leave it in the refrigerator until ready to use.
13. Spread cream cheese mixture over the cake, leaving ¾in (2cm) of cake empty on the far end.
14. Arrange citrus fruit evenly over the cream.
15. Roll up the cake using baking paper, like you would a nori roll.
16. Cover with baking paper and rest for 1 hour in a refrigerator.

*Double boil is a method to melt chocolate without burning. Place a bowl over a smaller saucepan filled with boiling water over low heat. Make sure the bowl is slightly bigger than the saucepan so it sits on top. This allows the steam to slowly melt the chocolate. Place chocolate in the bowl and continue to heat gently until chocolate has melted. If you have a fondue set you can use it. Don't let base of bowl touch the boiling water.

Green Tea-flavoured Chocolate Fondue

Ingredients
7oz (200g) white chocolate
1 teaspoon green tea powder
4oz (120g) thickened cream
variety of fruits in season, cut
  into small pieces

Utensils
knife, chopping board, mixing
  bowl, saucepan, wooden
  spoon, fondue pot, fondue
  forks or bamboo skewers

1. Chop chocolate on a chopping board, put into a mixing bowl and double boil* to melt chocolate.
2. Dissolve green tea powder in cream.
3. Add green tea and cream mixture to the melted chocolate mixture and stir gently with a wooden spoon to combine.
4. Serve over a heat (such as candle with a bowl-stand). Use forks or bamboo sticks to skewer pieces of fruit and dip into the melted chocolate.

*Double boil is a method to melt chocolate without burning. Place a bowl over a smaller saucepan filled with boiling water over low heat. Make sure the bowl is slightly bigger than the saucepan so it sits on top. This allows the steam to slowly melt the chocolate. Place chocolate in the bowl and continue to heat gently until chocolate has melted. If you have a fondue set you can use it. Don't let the base of bowl touch the boiling water.

Drinks

To complete your sushi party, why don't you prepare some authentic Japanese drinks?

Hot Drinks

Sen-cha (Common Green Tea)

(for 2 cups)

To prepare hoji-cha, place 1 tablespoon tea leaves in a teapot and add about 2 cups of hot water (ideally around 175–195°F/80°-90°C). Steep for 1 minute before serving.

Hoji-cha

Roasted green tea. It has slightly larger leaves than sen-cha green tea plus it has a roasted aroma. It contains less tannin and caffeine compared to other green teas.

For 2 cups

To prepare hoji-cha, place 2 tablespoons of tea in a warmed teapot and add about 2 cups of boiling water. Steep for 30 seconds before pouring and serving.

Genmai-cha

Genmai-cha is blended with hoji-cha and roasted rice grains, imparting a nuttiness to the tea.

To prepare genmai-cha, place two teaspoons of tea in a warmed teapot, add 2 cups of boiling water and steep for 30 seconds before pouring and serving.

Cold drinks

Green tea: Soak tea leaves overnight or for a couple of hours in water.

Mugi-cha (Barley Tea)

It does not contain any calories or caffeine, but the roasted aroma is loved by the people in Japan, especially in summer.

To prepare, you can follow the instructions on the packet or follow these instructions.

1 mugi-cha tea bag
36fl oz (1 litre) water

Bring water to boil in a saucepan, add mugi-cha and cook for 3-5 minutes to extract flavour by boiling.

Sushi Party

Sushi Party

When you feel comfortable about making sushi, you might like to share your new knowledge with your friends. You could start thinking about having a sushi party.

It takes some planning and preparation (as most parties do), but it could be lots of fun. Your guests can eat the sushi that you have made, or you could have a do-it-yourself party, where the guests make their own sushi—under your instruction, of course! Temaki-zushi (hand-rolled sushi) is most suitable for a do-it-yourself party. All the ingredients are set out on the table and guests just roll up their own sushi into small cone shapes and eat straight away (see the Maki-zushi party section).

You could even include a Sushi Cake (see recipes), which would be great for a special occasion such as a birthday or end-of-year celebration.

A few decorations on the table, such as origami napkin holders and chopstick holders and rests, along with some brightly coloured plates will add to the atmosphere.

Before your party, you should start thinking about how you want to decorate and serve the food. Sushi can look tempting on its own, but when it is arranged beautifully on a large plate with a few garnishes and decorations it looks irresistible.

If you are using a round plate or tray, it is best to start from the centre with some interesting, attractive sushi pieces such as futomaki or nigiri-zushi—maybe three stacked together. From there you can form patterns moving out to the edge of the plate. Think about the colours of the various fillings when making your design.

On a rectangular plate, you can start your design from the middle of one long side, and radiate sushi out from that point. You can continue to decorate the plate by adding some leaves cut into shapes, or one or two pieces of origami. If you have them in your garden, camellia, bamboo or aspidistra leaves are very good for this. The aspidistra leaves can be easily cut into interesting shapes with scissors. Just make sure you wash them well first (see Garnishes and Decorations in Basic Techniques).

Origami Paper Decorating Ideas

Chopstick Rest

makes 2 chopstick rests

You will need:

1 origami paper (approximately 6 x 6in/15 x 15cm, scissors

1. Cut origami paper in half with scissors.
2. Fold in half lengthways and fold in half again.
3. Using this strip, loop one end over and under to make a simple loose knot. Flatten the knot with your finger and thumb.
4. Repeat with other half of paper.

Chopstick Pocket

makes 1 chopstick pocket

You will need:

1 piece origami paper

1. Fold the origami paper in half.
2. Unfold to open. Fold the right-hand side in half again, towards the centre line.
3. Fold the left-hand side in half, towards the centre line and unfold. Fold the left corner towards the half-fold line and refold the left quarter to the centre line.
4. Fold the right top corner towards the half-fold line and fold the right side over along the centre fold line.
5. Turn it over and fold up lower part (about 1in/3cm).
6. Turn it over again and insert chopsticks in top pocket.

Napkin Holders

makes 6

You will need:

2 x origami paper (6in/15cm), double-sided tape

1. Cut origami paper into thirds.
2. Wrap strip around folded napkin. Secure in back with double-sided tape.

Name Plates/Tags

You will need:

small pieces of paper
bamboo sticks

On the paper you may write the names of dishes and, using a bamboo stick, insert it into one of the sushi. Alternatively, you can fold the paper to make small name plates to stand beside each variety of sushi, sauce or filling.

Hanging Paper Lanterns

Sometimes you can buy paper lanterns at craft or variety shops. To create a Japanese atmosphere for your party you could decorate these with Japanese writing. You can copy the writing in these pictures. The symbols mean 'sushi'. Then, you are not just making sushi, you are writing sushi too!

Noren with Origami Paper

Noren is a short split fabric curtain hung above the entrance to a Japanese restaurant and often seen in homes too. You could make a paper noren and hang it above the doorway in your home.

You will need:

About 6½ feet/2 metres string or ribbon to suspend curtain
10 pieces of square origami paper (6in/15cm)
glue stick

1. Make 2 panels by glueing 5 origami sheets end to end in a row.
2. For each panel, make a fold across one end, approximately ¾in (2cm) from the edge, depending on the thickness of string or ribbon being used.
3. Place the ribbon under the fold and secure the pocket with a glue stick, keeping the 2 panels close together. When dry, hang above a doorway.

Different Types of Sushi Parties

Maki-zushi Party

Maki-zushi is a great party dish. You need to spend time to prepare fillings, sushi rice and nori and set the table. Guests make the sushi by themselves, choosing their own fillings using small bamboo sushi mats.

Arrange plates and dipping sauce, accompaniments (pickled ginger, soy sauce) on the table. You can also add colourful plates to make the party more attractive.

Tips

- If you like, you may prepare some written notes on how to make maki-zushi rolls.
- Older kids may help younger children to make sushi as requested.
- Guests may choose whatever they like, but it may help to give some suggestions about combinations of colours and balance of ingredients before they choose their fillings.

Temaki-zushi Party

Host a sushi-making party, where everyone can make their own sushi. Prepare fillings and sushi rice and the essentials for rolling sushi and arrange on the area where you will be working.

For do-it-yourself rolls, it is better to prepare half or quarter-size nori so you can avoid slicing them. See Temaki-zushi section for more information.

Nigiri-zushi Party

At a nigiri-zushi party, you can be the sushi chef. Set your kitchen bench up like a sushi counter. Put a hachi-maki band (like a bandana) around your head and arrange ingredients in front of you. Take sushi orders from your guests, make it for them, and say 'Here you go', 'O-machi', or 'Yoh', as you put the sushi on their plate. Guests can then eat the sushi straight away. Alternatively, you can take it in turn to be the sushi chef making nigiri-zushi for each other. It is fun to see your friends making nigiri for you.

Today's Menu

Hand-rolled Sushi Cone
Have fun rolling your own temaki-zushi with nori, sushi rice, fillings and dressings below.

sushi rice, white or brown rice
cucumber
avocado
carrot
mustard cress
salad leaves
cheese
ham
smoked salmon
teriyaki chicken
teriyaki beef
homemade mayonnaise
cream cheese
sweet chilli sauce
wasabi (super hot! be careful!)

Party Food

Tomato Canapés
makes 4 pieces

Ingredients
3–4 teaspoons sushi rice
4 petite tomatoes
soy sauce jelly (see recipe)

Utensils
petite knife, chopping board, teaspoon, toothpicks (optional)

1. With a petite knife, cut tomato in half horizontally.
2. With a teaspoon, scoop out seeds.
3. Stuff with sushi rice and top with soy sauce jelly
4. Instead of jelly, you may use canned tuna with a little soy sauce.

Tomato Sushi
makes 4

Ingredients
4 petite tomatoes, such as amoroso
4 teaspoons sushi rice
2 teaspoons canned tuna
4 drops mayonnaise
white sesame seeds, roasted, for decoration
4 blueberries or 1 olive

Utensils
knife, chopping board, teaspoon, 4 toothpicks (optional)

1. With a knife, trim off the bottom of the tomato. This will make the tomato sit flat on the plate. If the tomato is oval-shaped, slice it in half horizontally and scoop out the seeds and add to the sushi rice.
2. Cut the top off and use it like a lid.
3. With the teaspoon, scoop out the seeds/inside of tomato and discard.
4. Put 1 teaspoonful of sushi rice inside the tomato cups and give a little press to set.
5. Decorate with tuna and a drop of mayonnaise.
6. Sprinkle sesame over mayo.
7. Arrange blueberries on top or spear blueberries with toothpick and stick through the tomato lid.

There are various options for toppings, choose whichever you like.

Roll Canapé
makes 8 pieces

Ingredients
¼ avocado, sliced
1 slice lemon, quartered
1 tablespoon canned tuna
2 school shrimp (prawns)
1 tablespoon cucumber,
    chopped
1 cherry tomato, halved
1 small slice prosciutto ham,
    cut in quarters
1 tablespoon ricotta cheese
pinch of mustard cress
one-third sheet nori
4oz (120g) sushi rice
mayonnaise, for decoration

Utensils
bamboo sushi mat, tezu (bowl
    of water), a knife, plate,
    chopping board

This is a plain hoso-maki roll, with a topping rather than a filling.

1. Prepare toppings.
2. Arrange nori lengthways on a bamboo mat.
3. Put sushi rice on the front left corner and with moistened fingers spread rice over nori sheet, leaving 1/3in (1cm) of bare nori at far end.
4. With the mat still covering nori, but not the rice-free portion of nori, hold rolling mat in position and press all round to make roll firm with fingers.
5. Lift up top of mat and roll over a little bit more to seal the joins.
6. With mat still in place, roll once more, and use fingertip pressure to shape roll in cylindrical form.
7. Cut into 8 pieces with a knife.
8. Place on a plate with cut edge facing up.
9. Arrange toppings as you like.

Sushi Cake

Ingredients

1 avocado

1 Lebanese cucumber

½ cup sushi rice (see Essential Ingredients for Sushi)

2/3oz (20g) smoked salmon

½ cup pink sushi rice (see Essential Ingredients for Sushi)

8 lime or lemon slices

1 teaspoon caviar

watercress, or other small green salad leaves

soy sauce, to serve

Utensils

round cake tin (8in/20cm) with removable bottom part, baking paper, large plate, rice spatula, peeler, knife, chopping board

makes 1 round sushi cake 8in (20cm) in diameter

1. Remove base of cake tin and use the outer wall as a mould. Place the bottomless tin on the centre of plate.
2. Line tin with non-stick baking paper.
3. Cut avocado in half and quarters. Deseed and peel. Slice them into crescents.
4. With a peeler, remove one strip of skin down the length of the cucumber and discard. With the peeler, continue to cut cucumber lengthways to make strips which will have just a little skin on the outer edge.
5. With a moistened shamoji, spoon half of the sushi rice into the tin and flatten evenly.
6. Place a layer of smoked salmon over the top of the rice.
7. Spoon pink sushi rice over the salmon and flatten evenly.
8. Layer cucumber strips over pink rice.
9. Top with the other half of sushi rice and flatten evenly.
10. In the centre, arrange smoked salmon to look like rose petals.
11. Arrange avocado slices in a radial pattern.
12. Insert lemon slices between avocado slices.
13. Decorate outer edges of avocado slices with caviar and small salad leaves.
14. Remove outer tin support.
15. Cut into slices using a knife moistened with a wet cloth. Serve with soy sauce. You may decorate with candles for a birthday celebration

Sushi Cake with Nori-maki

Ingredients

*1 Teardrop Roll in Flower
    Pattern (see recipe)*
½ Flower Roll (see recipe)
*½ Ebi-roll (Shrimp/Prawn Roll)
    (see recipe)*
choose any fillings you want
*choice of salad leaves, gari
    (pickled ginger) or fruit such
    as strawberries, blueberries,
    kiwi fruit, flower-shaped
    carrots, beetroot jam*

Utensils

*knife, chopping board, damp
    cloth, cake plate*

A cake arrangement using sushi rolls.

1. With a wet knife slice futo-maki to make 8 pieces and arrange them in a circular formation from the centre of the plate outwards.
2. Slice flower rolls into 4 pieces and arrange them on top of futo-maki in a circular formation from the centre.
3. Slice shrimp rolls into 4 pieces and arrange them on top.
4. Arrange gari, salad leaves, flower-shaped carrot and fruit around the cake to decorate.

Sushi Gift Box

A sushi box can make a wonderful and unusual gift. Arrange sushi in a simple cake box and decorate with origami. You could include a note about the ingredients and that you made it. However, you must make sure food is not spoiled by warm temperatures, so you need to keep it cool beforehand and advise that it should be eaten soon.

Sushi Picnic

Sushi is a convenient fingerfood for a picnic. However, if you use raw fish in sushi, you need to keep it cold. by storing it in a well-insulated cooler until ready to eat. Don't forget to take some soy sauce. For convenience you can buy sachets or small bottles from Japanese groceries. Wasabi could be included for older kids and adults. It is a good idea to take hand-wipes too.

Edamame is a great side dish with sushi for picnics. And fresh fruit is suitable for dessert.

Rather than preparing the sushi at home, you could bring all the ingredients and your friends can make maki-zushi at the picnic.

At the picnic, fillings can be kept in containers or arranged on large plates. Packed fillings and sushi rice in sealed containers are easy to carry. You might use a portable ice box, but it would be very impressive to carry some of them in a furoshiki. This is a traditional Japanese square cloth used for wrapping and carrying clothes, gifts or other goods. Furoshiki are usually attractively decorated, varying in size. Common sizes are 17¾in (45cm) to around 27½in (70cm). In Japan, lunch boxes are commonly wrapped with small furoshiki.

Assemble sushi in a round container/plate

This is a basic pattern once you used to do it you may arrange in your idea.

First of all decide where the centre of the plate is and place an attractive sushi piece in the centre, such as nigiri-sushi or a piece of futo-maki (thick roll). Arrange sushi pieces in a circular pattern of 360 degrees.

Haran

Varieties of sushi on platters or in lunch boxes are frequently separated by decorative leaves or bamboo dividers known as 'haran'. One you are probably familiar with is the small green plastic jagged leaf you find in sushi containers. If you want to include these in your own lunch boxes, you may find them at Japanese grocery stores. However, if you have aspidistra leaves, camellia or bamboo in your garden, wash them first and cut into shapes with scissors, to use as dividers or decoration.

Lunch Box

A typical Japanese lunch box (called a bento box) is a small box with several compartments, each containing a variety of interesting food, including sushi. With a bit of planning, you can prepare your own sushi bento box, like the one in the photo opposite.

A plastic container with compartments is suitable for arranging sushi as it keeps the pieces separate so the flavours don't mix, as well as creating a decorative effect.

Haran or baran is an ornamental lunch box divider shaped like grass, these days made of green plastic, though they used to be real leaves long ago. If you don't have a box with dividers, you could make your own by using paper or aluminium cupcake cases, or even cut decorative shapes from a washed aspidistra leaf.

Tips

Eating sushi with your fingers is acceptable, but you can bring disposable chopsticks or a fork with your lunch box. For lunch boxes, you should avoid using raw fish unless you can keep your lunch box in a refrigerator.

On a rectangular-shaped palate, you can decide on the front angle and arrange the sushi so it looks good when that angle is facing toward you.

Questions and Answers

Q1. Why is the rice sticking to my fingers?
Did you make sure to moisten your fingers before handling rice? If your fingers aren't wet, the rice will stick to your fingers very easily.

Q2. Why is the rice is coming out from the ends of my sushi roll?
Did you put too much rice on the nori? Make sure you only put the least amount of rice you need.

Q3. The filling isn't in the centre of the roll. What went wrong?

Make sure that you place the fillings in the centre of the rice before rolling (not near the edge of the mat).

Q4. Which side of the nori is front?
If you hold the nori under a good light, you can see there is a smooth side and a rough side. When rolling, place the rough side towards you and then once rolled the smooth side will be on the outside of the roll.

Q5. I can see the lines on the nori sheet. Where do these come from?
The lines originally came from the bamboo mats on which the sheets were made, when they were made by hand. Machine-made nori copies this pattern. Also, if you measure the nori sheet, it is not totally square. One side is slightly longer than the other.

Q6. How can I choose soy sauce for sushi?
There are many brands of soy sauce available in the shops. I recommend you choose natural brewed soy sauce, such as Kikkoman.

Q7. It is hard to slice nori roll. What can I do?
Always use a damp tea towel or kitchen paper and ask an adult to help you wipe the knife before slicing; it makes it easier to slice your sushi smoothly.

Q8. Can I eat sushi with my fingers?
Yes! Just make sure you wash your hands first.

Q9: What is 'sashimi'-quality fish?
Sashimi is a dish of raw fish. Not every fish on the market can be eaten raw. There are regulations in the fish markets to qualify fish for sashimi. It must be very fresh and kept at the correct temperature. Ask your fishmonger if you are not sure.

Index